#FutureOfWork

RESILIENT GROWTH PRINCIPLES

Prashant Pandey

White Falcon Publishing

www.whitefalconpublishing.com

Future Of Work: Resilient Growth Principles
Prashant Pandey

www.whitefalconpublishing.com

All rights reserved
First Edition, 2021
© Prashant Pandey, 2021
Cover design by White Falcon Publishing, 2021
Cover image source freepik.com

The contents of this book have been certified and timestamped on the POA Network blockchain as a permanent proof of existence. Scan the QR code or visit the URL given on the back cover to verify the blockchain certification for this book.

The views expressed in this work are solely those of the author and do not reflect the views of the publisher, and the publisher hereby disclaims any responsibility for them.

Requests for permission should be addressed to
prash.pandey@gmail.com

ISBN - 978-1-63640-310-6

"There are decades where nothing happens, and there are weeks where decades happen."
— *Vladimir Lenin*

FOREWORD
BY MUNISH MITTAL

FUTURE OF WORK

I have known Prashant for over half a decade now and his penchant for going to the depths of a subject matter is amazingly beyond description. Every time, his inquisitiveness has left me thinking, 'how I wish I could be so diligent and thorough'? My attention span fails and dwarfs me each time!

Timing for Prashant to pen down a bible on Future of work couldn't have been more appropriate. We are living in a socially distanced world and it perhaps is here to stay. Question isn't what new pandemic will strike our world, the question is when. Technology had already made geography a history. If the border controls and regulatory frameworks were to be more considerate, even more work will happen in distributed and remote fashion. At least, there is no blockers to thinking part of work not to be tied to location and all the old fashioned white collar work can been have increasingly getting acted upon from outsourced and off-shore centers. Crowd sourcing has been quite a successful phenomena rapidly being embraced by both innovators and legacy businesses in recent years, almost as the only way of doing business by the young entrepreneurs or 21st centenary. Mobile phone, cloud, social and AI, a.k.a. the Digital momentum has already redefined the experience, productivity, scalability, expectations and interactions of human beings and work environment. In this encyclopedia, Prashant has brought together a very thoroughly research interplay of forces and variety of considerations ranging from emotions, feelings, behaviour, culture to strategy, computer science and technology advancements in a very relevant and applied manner to reflect upon what and how the future of work would look like.

We exist only in the time dimension. In a grand galactic scheme of things, we live on a microscopic grain named planet Earth in one of the infinite blackholes. Work has been getting redefined since life happened perhaps a million years back on our planet Earth. Prashant has beautifully described our time travel through the Stone age to virtual reality. The human mind will get downloaded to a computer chip sooner than predicted. That is not important. Will we then be able to activate the power of human mind beyond the average of 10% today? And every minuscule increase in activation of minds thinking, information processing & storing faculty will transform our civilization. Prashant has beautifully crafted the relevance and applicability of a Data Driven decision making & infinite possibilities which will get opened up of our Quantum quest and how these have begun to redefine the present and future of work.

How much more Productive can we become, rather should we become? This is a serious question which will differentiate human beings from machines in the time to come. Would we afford more time with nature? Can we rejuvenate our soul doing more creative rather simple act of painting a canvas with water colours and rejoice? Prashant has very genuinely brought a comprehensive set of ideas together to make 'Future of work' serve as a guide for us to reflect upon and adopt to adapt in our constantly changing universe of earning livelihood.

I wish Prashant the very best and highly recommend challenging your thinking with these compulsive 'ideas to grow'!

Munish Mittal
Former CIO - HDFC Bank
Linkedin: https://www.linkedin.com/in/munishmittal10/

FOREWORD
BY ANDREW HASCHKA

Having spent many years working with Prashant in the IT industry, leading customers to transformative ways of working; it's clear his thought leadership has brought enormous value to organizations in the ways they grow and service their customers.

Prashant has built centers of excellence around digital transformation from building, evolving and promoting applications to their consumers. The Future of Work is clearly an ever changing and adapting journey by which we must navigate multiple paths and negotiate with numerous stakeholders. Prashant brings his experience to this book in engaging at an executive level to support the delivery of the solution. Leading by example and demonstrating these concepts in visual and interactive ways.

In defining a future state and strategy, the first aspect that should be well considered and documented is the current state and challenges to overcome. Prashant covers many aspects typically forgotten, however critical in the dependency mapping process and with high impact to transformation. Areas such as the digitization of real estate, dynamic changes to identity management, security, attire and connectivity. The expected state of corporate culture is shown to shift in time, format and task.

The tools we leverage to elevate our teams have cultural constraints and see impact from transformational leadership themes, dynamic delivery and integrated analytics. Code is everywhere and in every role from developers to executives; looking to optimize every aspect of the function we are driven to. Seemingly intangible concepts many years ago are now commonplace like serverless and automated processes. Evolving into physical execution through digital twin initiatives and processing faster than we ever thought possible with Quantum computing is becoming a common thought process in business strategies and growth projects.

Performance is able to be benchmarked and measured like never before: Leveraging changes to roles and functions resulting in improvements to revenue generating service lead time, deployment frequency and optimizing the time to restore in the event of failure. Even reducing the volume of failures themselves. Whilst we continue to re-learn the limits of technology, it's also pertinent to check in on the physical, mental and emotional exhaustion caused by overwork and stress. Staff burnout is becoming a more visible factor in organization effectiveness and we must adapt the usage of our staff differently to the use of our tools.

Once we look out from our microcosms to the city, country and planet we consume and inhabit; environmental impact is now also a key consideration and statistic boards will benchmark performance by. Offsetting carbon for solution inefficiencies has become a band- aid solution, but more so now we are driven to deliver solutions with lower impact on the environment in the first place.

Prashant's experience in delivering services to consumers digitally with efficiency and high impact is known in the market; and now demonstrated in this book. I hope you enjoy reading it and can gain the same insights from these words as I did.

Andrew Haschka
Linkedin: https://www.linkedin.com/in/andrewhaschka/

ABOUT THE BOOK

IN THIS URGENT, transformative and relevant book, Prashant sets out multiple viewpoints, their span spectrum and extremely important ideas for how the future of work will emerge and evolve to create and capture your effort's value, amplify authenticity and maximise your gains for years to come.

Prashant has spent years investigating and learning the cause and effect of technology on strategy, culture, and people, across continents. Based on his learning experience of working with hundreds of clients, cultures and industries across 40+ countries, he has shared salient ideas of what must be done in order to build your organisation's and your #FutureOfWork i.e. FOW.

He has shared his precious ideas in five parts in this book. Each of five parts have been further elaborated as chapters. Each chapter is a scale of "From" and "To". You will find that you will be at a different point on that scale compared to others, it's fine. *"Words of Wisdom"* at the end of each chapter are ideas that will make a difference in your life, when internalised.

In the first part, he articulates a crystal clear description of "**challenges**" that individuals, teams and organisations face today. In the second part, keeping "empathy" at the center, he focuses on *"feelings"* of people and groups. Often, "feelings" are missed out, but are the MOST important part of the future of work. In the third part, building on his ideas of innovation of time and space, *"structure"* of the future of work is explained. Once you build self-awareness after these learnings, the fourth part is the solution, *"tools"*. Tools that are available to reduce time, increase quality and reduce your cost of solving problems. Finally, he lays out *strategies*, to build your purpose for the future of work. He shares ideas not for defining the purpose of the employer, but employees, interns and future employees too. Remember, *purpose is more powerful than power itself.*

As Prashant makes clear, where we live, where we work and where we earn is disjoint, disconnected and disrupted. Building Future of work will not be simple and easy to do, but if you follow the ideas that he shares here, it is a goal certainly within your reach.

WHY THIS BOOK?

How to create #Future of work? Who creates people experience– IT, Employee, HR or Business? These are the questions which I heard hundreds of times from my clients. I read about them, I ran workshops around them, and then, I got an idea. Instead of writing a code, why don't I write a book? A book about resilient strategies of growth principles to take people and organisations from work to the future of work.

The context is that you and your organisation is going through the transformation, and there is not one, but many things that need to be disrupted and transformed to accelerate for the future of work. The problem is that your solution to the future of work is limited by the viewpoint of the person/team (HR/IT/LOB) who is chartered with fixing this problem. However, the right approach is to look at the problem of the future of work from multiple dimensions. These dimensions include challenges of work, feeling of work, technology for work, structure for work, and purpose of work. Next step is to understand the capability gap of the organisation in each of the dimensions and to create a journey map for transformation along these dimensions. This book is an effort towards bringing you multiple viewpoints and ideas that you need to consider in-depth to mediate your organisation's growth with the future of work.

Do you have a strategy to build your #Future of work? When this question needs to be answered, you need ideas. If you are a change agent, your choices, decisions, and insights will have direct implications on the rate of growth of the business, lives of people, and technology road map of people.

"Culture eats strategy for breakfast," a wise man once said. Irrespective of the part of the globe you are in when reading this book, cultural awareness, understanding this, and alignment are a must for executing your strategy for #Future of work. You need to look at the change from multiple viewpoints. You need to evaluate and design the change from multiple viewpoints.

But which dimensions should you be aware of while planning your #Future of work? This book is an effort to lay down the landscape of the dimensions you should be aware of first. Once you are aware of the dimensions, it is important to understand the characteristics of the dimension. Once both these steps are clear to you, you, as a change agent, can choose the change, the rate of change, and the need for change.

One shoe doesn't fit all. That is true even for #Future of work. Your #Future of work will be different than the #Future of work of others. But you need to be clear in your head regarding your reasons while setting the path of change. I tried to bring this fact together for you by adding "words of wisdom" from global experts in the respective section in this book.

This book will be an ideal guide that you can refer to during your and your organisations course of transformation to course correct your strategy of change.

So let's begin the change with the first step. Let's read about resilient principles..

CONTENTS

PART ONE

CHALLENGE

1

DIGITAL REAL ESTATE

From:

Real Estate: Since the evolution of work, human work is done by and for three things - hand, head, and heart. For example, in ancient times, the job of the messenger (hand) was to deliver the message (heart) of one person/king (head) to another person/ king (head). The challenges in the task of delivering a message have been the deformation of the quality of the message, the time taken to deliver the message, and the cost of delivering the message. These three challenges are equally applicable to any work that is done in your organisation. This example applies to transportation of not just messages, but any other thing, such as food, money, humans, goods, music, education, and ideas. Real estate was built around this work to make it easier, efficient, and better. These real estates were tangible and were classified as horses, buildings, tables, chairs, food for horses, etc.

To:

Digital Estate: Over the centuries and decades, technological innovation has played a crucial role in reducing the cost of work, increasing the quality of the work, and reducing the time taken to do the work. With the advent of computers, investment in technology also became part of real estate. This is what is known as *Digital Real Estate*. Investment in technology is also classified as tangibles investment. Networks, computers, devices, and data are most commonly described as digital real estate. The challenges in the "hand" part of the work challenge are significantly solved by digital real estate. For example, in the example of transportation of messages, the job of messenger is completely taken over by technology like computers and the internet. However, the "head" and the "heart" parts of the job are still primarily done by humans. The creation of music (head) and listeners of the music (heart) are still humans; however, the platform to transfer music (hand) is completely digitized. Your investment in the digital real estate is directly proportional to the growth of your music business. There has been a consistent effort to use technology to do the "heart" and the "head" parts of work too, but this progress has been relatively slow because of uneven investment. The growth path of an organisation should be able to adapt and adept to accept the digital real estate investment and evolution - the faster the better.

Words of wisdom:

Invest in digital real estate.

In your industry, classify the work done by and for head, heart, and hand. Investment in digital real estate for "hand" is the first step of #Futureofwork. The subsequent steps are investments in digital real estate for "heart" and "head". These investments are directly proportional to the evolution of technology.

2

IDEAL IDENTITY

From:

Real: *"Everything you can imagine is real"*, Pablo Picasso said once. Historically, humans have created ideas and put them on a canvas. Then, the canvas gets copied as a product, and voila, moments are created. Over the centuries ago, such moments have been created for objects as well as things. Telephone, car, airplane, rubber, bread, and many more (Reference: *Inventions That Changed The World*) have transformed the way humans work. One commonality amongst the identity of these products was **reality**. When the consumers consumed these products, the products were real, they were tangible, and they could be tasted and smelled. Mere invention of the typewriter was one large breakthrough as it helped the ideas to spread, in real life. The ideas from architects, writers, painters, policy makers, judges, and scholars got a canvas. These canvases were then copied and shared in the form of newspapers, journals, rulebooks, text books, and policy documents. Until very recently, people started using desktops, which were physical and were bound to their location in the office.

To:

Virtual: The canvases of consuming products have moved from physical to virtual. "Screen" is the reality now. There are different types of screens for different types of consumers. Before the consumer consumes the real product, they are going to consume the virtual version on screen. One commonality amongst the identity of products in #Futureofwork is **virtuality**. The ideas from the creators first get on a screen, and then, if needed, move forth to real products. Because everyone has a screen, everyone can see the virtual version of the product. If they like the virtual version, then, if possible, they can consume the real version. The creativity cycle of "idea to paper to real" will move to "idea to screen to real" in future of work. I am writing this book on an I-pad instead of a notebook or a piece of paper. The "virtuality" brings in the huge challenge of "fakes". The impact of fakes in virtuality is significantly higher than the impact of fakes in the real world. Imagine someone faking one's voice to login to the IVR of a bank account and transfer the money instantly. Imagine someone faking their identity on social media and sharing ideas in contrast to the belief of an individual, detrimental and poisonous. Even desktops have become virtual, not bound to a location or a seat in office, and can be consumed on "screen" of choice, which is a positive impact. While, on one side, "screen" virtuality will be the reality of future of work, the challenges of fakes will have become more prominent. The fakes will go beyond text or passwords all the way to face, voice, and *digital twins*.

Words of wisdom:

"Virtual" products delivered on "screen" will grow in future of work.

To grow to future of work, your product should be available virtually for consumers to consume. This virtual experience will impact the growth of your business and product. Futureofwork will have to ensure that the ideal identity of the virtual product is protected from fakes, especially digital.

3

INTERMITTENT INTERNET

From:

Intermittent: In 1960, with the creation of ARPANET (Advanced Research Projects Agency Networks), the first prototype of the internet was created. The purpose of the early internet was to transfer information from source to destination, quickly and safely. This purpose of transferring information was carried out on a "wired" medium for decades to come. With evolution of technology, the "quickness" of the rate of data transfer increased further and further. Then, one day, a magic happened- the information could travel "over the air" instead of wire - even at home. While, in the early 1970's, traces of wireless protocols could be found, Dr O'Sullivan is credited with inventing "wi-if". Late 1990s is the time when the wide and commercial use of "wi-fi" can be accounted for general "work" purposes. The slow growth of the internet in the early 40 years of its inception for work was significantly accelerated with advent "wi-fi" in the last two decades. *"Wi-fi is like oxygen"* - especially for the gen Z. It's ubiquitous, it's necessary, and it's ingrained in daily work and lifestyle. Sounds familiar? Agree? But you will be surprised to know that only around 4.57 billion, i.e., 59% of the world's population, is using the internet as of July 2020 (statistics report). On the contrary, a few institutions started to work on creating "free wi-fi" cities, schools, and work locations. The availability, accessibility, and accountability of internet significantly influence the work and the way it's done.

To:

Ubiquitous: Not only speed, but security of the information being transmitted on the internet has been a fundamental requirement of work. While there has been a multi-fold growth in the speed, the concern of security has not been resolved till date. It is mainly because of the fundamental way security is taken care of. The security design principle was simple - take the data, lock it with the key, send the key, and then send the data. If anyone steals the key, the data is at risk. Cyber security experts and researchers are concerned with recent development of quantum computing. They worry about the likelihood of "breaking" the existing cryptographic key using quantum computing. The race for *"quantum network"* for the future of work has already started. Once real, quantum networks not only solve the problem of quantity of data that can be transferred, but will also solve the fundamental security problem. As you noticed, wired internet took almost 40 years to mature, wi-fi took almost half of that time, as in nearly the last 20 years, it has become ubiquitous. "Quantum network" revolution and evolution for the future of work will be faster than that. However, one thing to be observed closely is how this will benefit and influence the lives of 31% of the world population who didn't have access to the internet in 2020. You will have to very clearly understand and map the internet accessibility of your consumers in the future of work.

Words of wisdom:

"Internet" will be an "integral" part of future of work.

The rate of consumption of the future of work outcomes/products will be directly proportional to the bandwidth and security provided by the internet. The design for future of work must incorporate the consideration of internet via which the products will be delivered to the consumers.

4

PRIVACY PROBLEMS

From:

Persuasive: **Persuasive technology** is defined as the technology that is designed to change the attitude or behaviour. Technology was created as a tool to solve the problems faced by human beings. These tools were reactive in nature for solving the problem of work. For example, writing ledgers in the bank was tedious, so typewriters and computers were used. These typewriters or computers were used by humans when the problem of writing data required a reactive solution. The typewriter never proactively started typing the data unless it was triggered by human actions. The whole control to get the work done using technology was in the hands of humans, or more precisely, the minds of humans. While lots of data was entered in the digital world by humans, the brain to analyse the data that triggers human action did not exist. In the 1990's, BJ Fogg from Stanford University coined the term persuasive technology. This technology was intended to move the human behaviour towards work from reactive to proactive. For example, e-mail is a great example of a proactive technology trigger for work. An e-mail generates the same emotions in human beings that predators used to invoke in caveman. Since the proliferation of application of persuasive technology since early 2000, humans have been used as products. Products prompted by machines to take proactive actions to make profit by consuming digital products. Ever noticed who wishes you happy birthday first - your partner or you insurance company via e-mail? However, analysis of over two decades of data of an individual captured by the digital world by machines and actions taken to change behaviours of humans has caused significant threats.

To:

Proactive: Nations have started devising discussions, laws, and governance models to protect the privacy data of their citizens. In 2020, awareness about the volume of data captured and its implications on human behaviour and countries has tremendously increased. Research and trends clearly show that the behaviour of Gen, Zisseverely and negatively impacted by the lack of ethics around the use of persuasive technologies. *The Dark Web* has incurred billions of dollars of financial losses to the governments. The penalty cost on breach of consuming privacy data of individuals is meagre when compared to the profits that businesses can make from such data. Growth of technology, governance to protect data, and its economic benefits will be more coherent in future of work. The ethical, geographical, and economical models of your future of work should incorporate the privacy definitions of digital real estate.

Words of wisdom:

"Privacy Problem" will be solved by "proactive solution" designs in future of work.

The future of work will have plethora of data about human's environments of operations, devices being used by them, modes of logins, applications being consumed by them, and inter-connectivity of the devices. Digital experience measurement systems will drive experience beyond engagement, which will be governed by new governance and economic policies.

5

(SUPER) HUMANS

From:

Humans: Situation, problem, and solution - Since human evolution, this was the systematic cycle of innovation and problem-solving. The human brain and behaviour are quite aware of the situation they are in or are observed; they realize the problem in that situation. More importantly, human behaviour was also able to analyse whether the problem is worth fixing. And voila, there is a solution. For example, when banking started almost two centuries ago, humans were writing the ledgers on paper. They observed the problem that keeping a paper record is cumbersome, hard to transport, and more importantly, prone to weather conditions. The solution - the record book became electronic from paper. It was easy to keep the electronic records, transport could be handled using e-mail, and business contingency plan took care of the preservation of the books under different weather/natural conditions. This was the world where humans started keeping their observed behaviour in electronic form - in the digital world. One-way traffic. Humans were writing data in the digital

14

world and reading it at their wish. But did you realize when the digital world "automatically" started sending you e-mail notifications?

To:

Super Humans: Situation, problem, solution, **insights, and actions** - The systematic cycle of innovation and problem-solving got complemented by two more steps. These steps are complementary steps taken by machines. However, this is not the problem. The problem is that the machine feeds those actions back to humans. Hence, the loop of problem-solving becomes recursive and never-ending. As the digital world has lots of data written by humans, the machines have got the intelligence to analyse those data (develop insights). Those insights provide machines the power to take action. These actions are of two types. The first type of action is that the machine itself is able to solve the problem. For example, the air-conditioner keeps the room temperature (temperature chosen by human) constant on its own. The second type of action is that machines provoke humans. The machines provoke humans either to inform them about the situation or to seek help in solving the problem. When provoked, human goes through the same biological simulation that they used to go through when they saw a threat in a cave during the Stone Age. In Stone Age, this used to happen once in a while. Now, humans are simulated to these triggers many times in a single day, or rather in an hour. On one side, machines will solve the problem, and on the other, they will change human behaviour. Your future of work will have to draw the line and take care of native human creativity.

Words of wisdom:

"Human Avatars" will become prevalent and proliferate in future of work.

The future of work will have two types of tasks. Tasks that can be done by machines and tasks for which machine will need humans help. You will have to break the work into these categories. Ratio of both types of tasks will have to be measured and modified continuously.

PART TWO

FEELINGS

6

SPACE SENSITIVE

From:

Within walls. Humans do three kinds of work - **they learn, they think, and they act.** "Act" is the work that has always generated revenue for individuals, organisations, and industries. To generate huge revenue, it was clear that a huge number of humans have to act together. They act together not in time, but in space too. At the beginning of the 20th century, the industrial revolution set the stage for this synchronous and synonymous act. The creation of the railroad and the railway bogies that run on top of them was possibly the first indication where humans were brought together in the same space, within a wall, to do the same kind of work. Think of each wall as boxes. Each box had inputs, on which humans would act and generate outputs. The output of one box was interconnected to the input of the other box. Soon, it was realized that if we have to scale the boxes where people act, we also have to scale the people who can learn those acts and people who can think about the profitability of those acts. The evolution of the public learning system under the space of the wall was set to produce the workforce. Also, the universities under the wall were set to create minds who could think about the profitability of those acts. In short, there were many spaces defined by their walls and expected inputs and outputs.

To:

The world is the wall. The digital industry defined those walls as "cubicles" at the beginning of the 21st century. Keeping the tradition of the industrial era, in the digital era, people had to come every day to the defined wall (cubicle), act for a certain duration, and then go back home. However, the interesting part was that the act of thinking became more prominent than the act of actions as far as generating revenue is concerned. At the beginning of the 20th century, the wealth creators were big factories, but at the beginning of the 21st century, the wealth creators were information technology companies. The wall is broken now. The cubicle has come to the coffee table, the cubicle has come to the couch, the cubicle has come to the corner shop. The silos of walls of boxes are broken, and the wall is the wall created by the availability of oxygen. Humans started learning from every part of the world, while the teachers are in other parts of the world. Humans started thinking in the corner of their space where they are most comfortable, while millions of people started reading about those thoughts from the space they are comfortable with. Humans started working from the space, which is most comfortable and is acceptable to the organisation to deliver the goods that they are supposed to deliver or generate. While the workers started saving money for commute, the time of travel, and quality of family life, organisation started to tap into resources not limited by space, boundary, and wall. Your future of work and the legacy perimeter will be broken.

Words of wisdom:

"Space boundary" of your future of work is limited by "your freedom of thoughts".

The future of work will allow humans to work from the space where they are most productive. There will be three kinds of space: space to learn, space to discuss, and space to generate outputs. Space to discuss will be defined by the organisations, while the spaces to learn and generate output will be defined by humans who work in those organisations.

7

LOCATION LIMIT

From:

Early civilisation started by the side or river. Following the same pattern, during the industrial era of work, the society flourished near the centre of action. **"Centre of action"**referred to the places where the decisions were taken that could impact the financial status of the organisation. For example, New York, London, San Francisco, and Paris were few of the locations where the decisions were taken for businesses. It was also true that, not only decisions, but these locations attracted lots of people for work too, as the rewards were higher for working in these locations. On the other side, because of the influx of people to work on these locations, the balance of demand and supply became uneven. This made the cost of staying in these locations expensive. The cheapest alternative was suburbs. The locations for work started to be known as "downtown" (or "uptown" in few cases), while the place of stay for workers and their family was called suburb. Also, these "Centres of action" were like islands across the globe - not very well connected. So, not only people travelled from their suburb to

"Centre of actions" for work, but people also started travelling beyond "Centre of action" locations to drive the growth of business. Think of this model as a "star topology" of networks which is connected to suburbs, and there are many star topologies of "Centres of action" like that.

To:

With the advent of digital technologies in early 2000, not only the barrier of **"location limit"** was broken, but the business also started to become nimble and agile. People who used to commute to work on these "Centres of action" started saving their time in travel and devoted that time towards their productivity. Also, the advent of the digital revolution added "Centre of action" on global arena, like Hong Kong, Singapore, Shanghai, Bangalore, Tokyo, and Armenia, to name a few. However, this time, there was a huge advantage - the advantage that these "Centres of action" were connected by the "internet", which was affordable, secure, and accepted as a stepping stone in almost all leading businesses or industries. The topology mostly changed from "star" to "mesh" or, in some cases, "ring". Organisations started to use this phenomenal power of quick decision-making to understand, analyse, and decide the right location for right work and right cost. However, the maturity and adoption of this model is in direct proportion to the investment of that industry in digital technology. For example, financial institutions were one of the most early and high spenders in digital technology (after defence), and are leading the work model for the future of work. In consumer space, retail giants have spread their wings across the globe in connecting the consumers and producers instantly. The future of work will be limitless.

Words of wisdom:

Your future of work should leverage opportunity of "limitless location".

The future of work will free organisations to consume and produce products from any locations. These location choices will depend on cost advantage, the demand of the product, and agility of catering to the client needs instantly. Agile and nimble will be the outcome of long-term growth of your business.

8

CREATIVE CRAFT

From:

Limited reach. Ken Robinson, in his famous TedTalk, said that education is killing creativity. As industrialization accelerated in the beginning of 1900, the need to create a workforce to work in those industries also increased. Hence came the schools. These schools created curriculum, rather prioritised the curriculum that were suited to limit the people's creativity so that the number of people who could work in industry can be increased. Majority of the workforce that came out of the education system and was highly respected spent their time in creating "tools", mainly mechanical in nature. Tools to solve the problem of the industrial nature of work. The authentic creativity, like music, art, writing, and painting was broadly limited by two facts - one that the educational system was driving the behaviour of humans to be ready to work rather than being creative, and second that the authentic creativity had **limited reach**. Limits drawn by the media or channel on which it could ride. For example, good music can reach only those people who could attend the theatre, and similarly, a good painting can reach people who could visit an art gallery in their vicinity, provided there was an art gallery in that society or city. But the million dollar fact is - the tools created by these geniuses of the 19th century helped others to work efficiently, helped them to travel quickly, helped them to reduce the time taken to do their work. The intent of creating the tool was right, but the outcome was limited to the benefits of industrial work.

To:

Outreach. The digital era carried forward the trend, behaviour, and cycle of learning and creating tools. The only change was that, instead of mechanical engineering, lots of people started learning electrical/electronic engineering. And because they studied computer engineering, they started creating tools using silicon instead of iron. However, in the parallel universe that evolved as part of digital evolution,the technology was available not only to organisations but also curious, creative, and inquisitive humans who were not working in these organisations. This universe had broken the barrier of "limited reach" and allowed creativity to **"outreach"**. The authentic creations, suited for the human needs, got adopted quickly, smoothly, and swiftly. In some cases, even the governance of the nation was not prepared for adoption of such authentic creativity and had to chase the rule creation. The digital world observed neo rich who were unconventional in their education style, authentic in creativity, and had leveraged the power to outreach beyond dreams. These are the leading indicators of the power of future of work - outreach.

Words of wisdom:

"Authentic Creativity" will outreach in future of work, when crafted well.

The future of work will simplify technology. The simplification will be to a point that technology will be consumed seamlessly by humans. Creative human souls, minds, and hearts will flourish beyond imagination of governance, economics, and geo-politics in future of work.

9

DRESS DILEMMA

From:

Uniform. The purposes of dress are: hide the body, communicate social status visually, and provide comfort to the body for the work that one is doing. Evolving human's dress also evolved over a period of years and needed to cater to either of three purposes of dressing. One fact that always persisted was that "A human is ideally part of three entities - oneself, team, or an organisation." As the concept of organisation evolved, the need for visual uniformity also grew. Hence came *"uniform"* - the dress that was the same for every human in all organisations of similar type. Armies, schools, manufacturing industries, and healthcare are great examples of workspaces where uniforms are mandatory. It was also observed that each clan or organisation's head had to dress differently so that he could be easily recognised. So, the heads of the organisations had historically been dressed with crowns made up of feathers, to thrones made up of diamonds, to the tie and pins that are subtly ostentatious. So, while the heads may or may not have uniforms, they certainly were dressed differently and wilfully than most of the people in their organisations. This practice was also related to the fact that the industrialisation required more human capital than more knowledge capital to drive profit in the organisation. Hence, the status was socially defined and standardised by the dress.

To:

No uniform. As "the world" is becoming "office" more and more, as the knowledge and authenticity are becoming a source of profit more and more, as the organisations are becoming private and profitable more and more, the concept of dress is moving from uniform to **non-uniform**. You can already see that the schools all around the world have started trends of moving to non-uniform from mandatory uniform. With the transformation of mechanical industry to knowledge industry, the heads of the organisations are dressing less ostentatiously but uniquely. They show their consistency, their authenticity, and drive the message of credibility by knowledge than by visuals. Don't you see the contrast in the way a CEO of a large firm used to dress two decades ago to how the CEO of a large firm dresses today? Future of work is bringing casual and comfort dress approach, so that people can be free to acquire and apply knowledge to work. Wherever knowledge flows, it brings freedom. The freedom to dress is one of the primary freedoms for an individual. At the same time, the individual should communicate the culture of the organisation. This entails that, in the future of work, more and more individuals will work in the organisations that are aligned to their values, culture, and knowledge.

Words of wisdom:

"Freedom to dress" is "future of work".

The more knowledge-oriented work is done by your organisation, the higher will be the outcome and value generated by your organisation. Dress dilemma will be a topic that you must have to consider to drive productivity, creativity, and authenticity in your "future of work".

10

ORIGINAL OUTCOMES

From:

Moon Industry. Richard R. Nelson, in his world-famous speech "Moon vs. Ghetto", has very clearly articulated the impact of unevenness of investment on society, technology, and work. As you know it's the outcome of the vote that counts, not the vote itself. Historically, when the nations grew and the world was limited by the capability to travel and migrate, the nature of work done in a nation was directly proportional to the direction of investment for outcomes in that country or organisation. For example, the nations where the government prioritised space mission more than the people's life for their pride, the work opportunities to work on space missions were highly paid, respected, and recognised compared to the work of saving lives of humans and the earth itself. This was in contrast to nations where the government prioritised human lives more than the moon mission. An individual is always inspired by he most recognised work that is done in his time. For more ian half the century, while the "moon" industry has sucked) lots of capital and tax of the nations, the results are far from tangible for the human lives staying on the earth. It would be fair to say that the moon industry is a solution to a problem, which does not exist.

To:

Sustainable Life. In the future of work, humans will be more aware about the evolution of technology, its impact on nature, and the outcomes of the efforts of an organisation on making human lives better. Already, the race to the moon by bleeding the earth has been replaced by saving human life and the earth. You can already see the pledge from most of the leading organisations to become carbon neutral in the coming decades. I saw an article that was talking about the trade-off of bitcoin vs. the amount of power the bitcoin technology consumes. These discussions were not very prominent around centuries ago as the awareness of the impact of the outcome on nature, related research study, and the reach of those researches was limited. All these problems have not already been solved by knowledge and the digital world, but have also accelerated the millennials' expectations from the organisations of the future of work. If you are one of the first companies in the world who made cars that ran on diesel, in the future of work, you will certainly have to think on how that car can run on sustainable fuel, like solar or hydrogen. Else the workers of the future of work will very likely not buy your car. This is a great example to demonstrate that how the outcome that your organisation will generate will be enticing the future of work workers - both to build your product and to buy your products.

Words of wisdom:

"Sustainable Outcome" is "future of work".

The closer the outcome of your organisation is to sustainability of earth and human, the more is the chance of your success and growth. You need to think deeply and decide where in the sustainability cycle of earth your organisation's outcome fits and contributes. This thought will decide the tenure, type, and tenacity of the people who will work in future of work.

PART THREE

STRUCTURE

PART THREE

STRUCTURE

11

ORGANIZED ORGANISATION

From:

Chain of command suits those organisations where decision-making is central and tasks done by workers don't need critical decision-making. This system as established because the work done by the users is homogeneous, predictive, and consistent. This also helped drive consistent behaviour amongst the community. The evolution of this type of organisation can be seen since the evolution of human society. But a more detailed structure in this organisation evaluation phase came in with "armies". They were the first large group of people working in the organisation and were the most organised. Industrial revolution industrialised the mechanical tasks. These industries learnt a lot from the existing organisational behaviours from armies. And they further refined and sharpened it. This was done by research, application of tools/management techniques and adjusting them over a period of time. For the industrial world,theories were devised with numbers like a community group larger than 150 people are ineffective and 7 is the ideal number of people that a single human should manage for effective productivity and employee experience. Total quality management (TQM) is a great example and is still used widely.

To:

Shadow organisation. Two things started to happen at the beginning of the digital age. First,the precise and defined tasks were transferred to machines. Second, the decision-making started to become decentralised. The organisation's decision-making power to individuals started moving from central to end employee based on the maturity of the organisation and adoption level of technology. Knowledge economy will move this shift more prominently in coming years and will change the organisation structure that was suited for industry and will make it more human-friendly, client experience-centric, and outcome-based. Arsene Wenger, the famous coach of Arsenal football, who wrote "my life in red and white", said that, *"it is the individual player who makes the difference, we as managers take a lot of credit that we do not always deserve"*. You can learn from football games. It is a one of the greatest examples of decision-making that needs to be done at the individual employee level of the organisation, while the group of employees have to cohesively work as a team towards the common goals. You must be thinking, yes that's right. But how that can be built at future of work scale. Concept of "Shadow organisation" is your answer. In the future of work, you will have to ensure that every employee is crystal clear on the goals of the organisation and is decisive enough to work towards creating value to the organisation. Behaviour of "shadow organisation" will help the individual workers get things done in the future of work.

Words of wisdom:

"Future of work" organisation will move from "structured" to "shadow" in continuum.

More "structured" your organisation is, more the chances of the work to be done by "machines". To harness the knowledge of humans for your profits, let the shadow organisation grow for future of work. Empower workers with intended behaviours so that they can take decide what the correct action is. Create "flowcharts" of decision-making for "future of work".

12

TACTICAL TASKS

From:

Incremental. Tasks are units of work that generate desired outputs. Predictive tactical tasks will generate incremental growth, provided the friction does not change. Einstein once said, *"Insanity is doing the same thing over and over again and expecting different results"*. A car manufacturing organisation is a great example of this. The tasks are calculated and scaled, and generate a predicted number of cars, unless the machine fails. You increase the resources that perform tactical tasks and the outcome/profit increases. This formula has been delivered with a fair amount of predictability in the past and in the industrial revolution phase. Such incremental growth based on tactical task prediction methodology has one limitation. The limitation is that prediction of growth is limited by the number of years that humans can take into consideration when taking decisions. Very likely, this duration is three years. The blindness to the evolving competitive landscape to reduce the time to do the task or disrupting the way the task is done immediately puts the growth plan of your organisation in peril. In worst case scenario, the industry or the organisation will cease to exist, unless they respond to the friction or the change. But if you don't have the resources to respond to the change, your organisation will perish.

To:

Transformative or disruptive. The tasks done in the knowledge-based future of work will have a proportional mix of incremental and transformative. Disruption in tasks will be done by either a new organisation or the organisations that are still agile enough to transform in the way tasks are done. For example, running a car by "electricity" or alternative sustainable source would required existing organisation to transform the way their task is done. Alternatively, a new organisation will come to challenge the way tasks were done to generate output. As I said, you can have workers in the organisations in the ratio of 80:20 (or something that suits your resource pool) to do increment vs. transformative or disruptive tasks. Incremental (80%) workforce will do the work that will be like counting the chicken. Whereas, 20% of the workforce will do the transformative or disruptive work that is like hatching the egg. Make sure not to count the eggs before they are hatched. This ratio of workers will provide you a knob that can be tuned based on the changing friction landscape in the future of work. The transformative or disruptive workers will get you the pulse of the needs well in advance as they are supposed to be tracking it from clients. Future of work tasks will not stay the same for three to five years, but the nature of tasks might change in six months, depending upon headwind.

Words of wisdom:

"Future of work" tasks done by humans will shift from "tactical" to "transformative" or "disruptive".

Your future of work should have the good ratio of "tactical" tasks and "transformative" tasks, say 80:20. Tactical tasks will generate predictive outputs, while transformative tasks will provide an edge against competition. Factor the ratio of the tasks based on your resource planning for future of work.

13

NINE TO FIVE

From:

Time-bound. 35 hours, 40 hours, 44 hours - a week. These are numbers that crop up when search is done for the amount of time one worker should dedicate. While this quantitative data is a great operational measure, it doesn't account for quality. No two humans can generate the same results working for the same amount of time, unless it's either a math textbook question or the work is replaceable by machine. Two reasons can account for this. First, the industrialisation of work didn't have the need for people to work from anywhere. Second, the management theory, which followed quantification of effort, only incorporated tangible metrics. The effect of weather, the effect of time of sunrise and sunset on human behaviour, and the understanding of human's mindset and emotions were left out of the quantitative calculation. While it did help the organisations to define a salary structure and work schedule, it didn't really allow the organisations to empower the employees to do the work that is most effective.

To:

Result-bound. A developer should be focused more on writing code than doing meetings, a salesman should be meeting customers and closing business rather than filling the operational data in the system. The behaviour design of the organisation in future of work will empower employees to do the right thing at the right place and right mood. Biologically, the creative capability of humans slows down with the direction of the sun during the day. The future of work will not force humans to do meetings in the morning and create architectural design or strategic plans in the evening, but very likely will give them the freedom to create the design with beer or at a place where the person is most creative and engaged. I noticed a gardener today taking a picture of himself while watering the plant. He was going to send that picture to his boss stating that he has done the job and plants look green. He said that he is not going to fill an excel sheet or time sheet to get his salary. Future of work will provide us tools that can measure the tangible and the intangible outcomes. Future of work is incorporating the behaviour design approach to ensure that the employees are doing things from a place and time where they are most comfortable with. Learning organisations are clearly stating the objectives and timelines to the employees. They are not measuring how long the employee worked in a day, but how much they generated at the end of quarter against the set objectives.

Words of wisdom:

"Future of work" will empower people to work "anytime".

Future of work will reduce the micromanagement of time of work, but will focus on larger issues like behavioural happiness of employees and empowering them by stating the objectives and timeline.

14

REALITY VIRTUALITY

Real Presence. What one can't see, can't manage. This mindset grew and got stronger as the organisations grew during the industrial era. If one is not physically present in the workspace, one can't be managed, and hence, one can't be productive. This hypothesis instilled and drove the behaviour of "real presence" of humans in the workspace. During a war, the soldiers had to be physically present. On the workshop floor, the worker had to be physically present. Not only chariot, even in the car, the driver had to be physically present to drive. Physical presence of humans not only brought the challenge of paying their salary, but also ensuring their well-beingand security, and reducing their health risk. "Occupational hazard" remediation became the responsibility of the organisations to ensure that their employees are safe and healthy. Mining, railroad, oil and gas, and defence are examples of the industries that started facing growing challenges of adopting "ethical behaviour". The growing awareness of human rights and negative impact of the working conditions put pressure on the organisations to focus their attention around the physical, mental, and social health of the employees. This prompted the behaviour of adoptions of "robots" in work and outsourcing of the work to the countries where the governance law was conducive.

To:

Virtual Presence. *"All the world's an office"*. Virtual became real since the industrial era was taken over by the knowledge era. Couple of decades ago, the early adopters and leading organisations started showing this behaviour. For example, the battle ground started seeing unmanned aerial and ground workforce. The shop floor started seeing machines sorting the clothes with very few texture differences. And needless to say,unmanned cars became a reality of which you all are aware. But the most critical innovation was the power to communicate - virtually. For humans, communication is the key. They communicated in three modes: one to one, one to group, and one to many. Collaboration tools starting from email, and then, ranging from Yahoo messenger, Jabber, Avaya, Polycom all the way till Zoom and Whatsapp changed the mindset that employees can communicate with each other virtually. This was a huge milestone and tipping point of change of mindset and behaviour. The future of work leading behaviour instilled the fact that "employee presence" could be virtual. Virtual employees can be managed. Virtual employees can deliver outputs. This trend is not only leading, but has been adopted and time tested. During 2020, this mindset got proven to the world that future of work is ready for virtual presence. Future of work has given opportunities to the organisations to create a global virtual office.

Words of wisdom:

In "Future of work" employee "virtual" presence will increase.

Future of work will accept,adopt, and accelerate the "virtual" presence of employees. Organisations will have capability to not only conduct virtual one to one meeting, but also one to small group (like boardroom) and one to many (keynote conference) communication virtually.

15

HOLD HIRE

From:

Hire for a lifetime. How long does an employee work for an organisation? What are the median years of tenure of employees in an organisation? If you measure that for yourself and your organisation, you will see these numbers decreasing over a period of time in history. Historical companies, when creating products that are incremental enhancement than their previous version, when the products are created at the same place, and the consumer market segment is incrementally grown, hire employees for a lifetime. The longer the tenure of these three elements for an organisation, the longer is the lifetime of the employees in the organisation. Hospitals in a community, schools in a society, and media group of a nation/ community are good examples of these types of organisations. Because the growth requirement and product requirement is incremental, the skill upgrade required for employees is also incremental. This is achieved by planning and educating employees on those skills and keeping them as part of the organisation for long-term and duration. In short, employees were hired, groomed, and grown for the lifetime of the organisation.

To:

Hire for timeline. Every industry has been either transformed or disrupted by rapid adoption of technology. Technology is not only ensuring that the products are made in reduced time, but also ensuring that the cost is less and quality is at par or higher than the man-made products. In many cases, technology is creating the products and services in a completely new way that is disruptive. The entertainment, advertisement, and education industry are few examples that have been transformed upside down in the last two decades. The survival of the fittest is putting organisations under tremendous pressure to up skill their employees at an unprecedented pace. This unprecedented pace becomes so fast most of the time that it becomes impossible to up skill the employee. In that case, the organisations choose to *rent* employees rather than *retain* employees. In the manufacturing industry, vertical integration saw outsourcing of products and components over centuries. The knowledge industry has seen an analogy of this outsourcing of employees. Over recent decades, employees are not outsourced, but outsourcing of complete functions has become routine phenomenon. Functions like hiring employees, financial documentation, and the development of code based on designs have been commonly outsourced. The position of the organisation's capability and skill on the continuum of cost of work on one side to skilled experts to do that work on the other side decides the tenure of an employee in the organisation. The higher the pointer to the right side, the longer will be the duration.

Future of work will instead see short projects with agile development cycle to drive the demand at an accelerated pace. This will drive the need for hiring people based on the duration of a project instead of lifetime.

Words of wisdom:

In "Future of work",average employee tenure will reduce to 3-5 years.

Future of work will empower employees with authentic skills. At the same time, it will drive the behaviour of hiring small project-oriented employees for the duration of the projects. While organisations will hire employees for projects, they will also work in organisations by their choice.

PART FOUR

TOOLS

16

INTEGRAL INTANGIBLE

From:

Quantity. Two ways to reduce the time to get the work done are - make the worker efficient and adopt a tool. The benefit of the purchase of a tool by any organisation has historically been evaluated by Return on Investment (ROI) calculation. The value of the number of tools purchased to reduce the cost was the fundamental reason for investment in the tool. Because the calculation was done before the purchase of the tool, two factors missing in the value evaluation of the tool included the quality of output of the software tool and the intangible value that the tool provided. Had the quality of the software been fabulous at release 1.0, there would not have been a release 10.0 of the same tool. As there were few vendors providing the tool of scale and the investment was done with 3-5 years horizon in mind, the money was paid upfront to the vendor for three- or five-year contract. This was called a perpetual model. The benefit of this model to the organisation was that the upcoming new releases of software were available to the organisation for an upgrade. At the same time, if the choice of tool is not appropriate especially when compared to the competitive organisation, the risk is significantly higher than the outcome and the efficiency of the organisation will be degraded compared to the competition. The challenge of buying software in this way was that the evidence of "intangible values" of human's experience was missing.

To:

Quality. With the proliferation of GenZ and millennials defining the value and success of the digital tools, the focus shifted from the quantity to the quality of the tool. The three qualitative and intangible parameters of the tool that became prominent for the future of work are human experience, sustainability, and availability. The intangible value of experience is defining how successful the tool will be in the organisation after adoption. The sustainability parameters like power consumption and carbon emission rating of the next generation tool are becoming more important for the organisation and employees of the future of work. The next-generation applications and digital tools are built using agile methodology and not the waterfall model. This is allowing the consumers of the tools to subscribe to the tool on a need basis. Because of the fact that the freedom to choose and quality started defining the intangible value of the tools, the future of work will be driven a lot by the quality of intangible values provided by the tools. Let's take a small example of logging into the desktop. Two decades ago the user name and password were the only and most secure way to log in. With time, the security and additional tools like multi-factor authentication token or dongle were added to the design. As you can see, the vertical integration of these two tools has certainly increased the security, but it was a significant compromise on the user experience. Imagine you are a bank and your clients have to log in using this cumbersome two-step process. Instead, the bank of the future will allow authentication like biometrics or certificates to reduce this intangible login experience of the client. This might sound small, but will be a significant factor in deciding which bank is the best bank of the future. Look around and observe how next generation is using technology and digital tools? Is it the same as you used the technology and digital tools? If you deeply reflect on this, your answer will definitely be 'No'. You will observe that next generation's future of work will value quality, simplification, and agility in the tool. Also, they would like to have freedom to choose, not every three years, but every month.

Words of wisdom:

In "Future of work", tools will be built keeping "empathy" at centre.

Future of work tools will prioritise intangible values of empathy, sustainability, and experience. The adoption and lifetime of the tool will be driven by these values. These values will be measured at a granular level of day or months, instead of a year or three years.

17

DATA-DRIVEN

From:

Telescopic. Until the telescope was invented in 1608, the astronomers used to observe the stars and planets using naked eyes. Using the measuring instruments, they used to record the position of the planets relative to the stars. As per the records, while the credit of the invention and patent of the telescope goes to Hans Lippersey, Galileo was equally important in ensuring that the telescope was used by the astronomical community. By the adoption of telescopes, do you think there were jobs of earlier astronomers that could be made less redundant? Yes, there were. But, at the same time, I am sure there must be astronomers who would have adapted quickly to leverage telescopes to their benefit and accelerate the innovation and decision-making of the astronomical community. This invention of the early 17th century was a stepping stone for enlightening mankind about how little they knew about planets and stars. And also to make them realise that, if they save the data and don't waste time on re-collecting it, they could progress faster and further in their understanding about astronomy without reinventing it. The last two centuries have seen significant enhancement in types of telescope (even to a point that telescopes are sent to space). Not only did these inventions help to see the space better, they helped in better collection of the data about space. Our understanding about space and planets in the last three centuries has grown manifold compared to the era of "naked eyes". But the question is, does your organisation have analogous data about the clients to whom your organisation sells products?

To:

Datascopic. Future of work will be fuelled by data. What a telescope did to astronomy, data will do that to the future of work. More the data, merrier the decision-making is. Machine is learning these data and using artificial intelligence to make decisions. As years progress, as decades progress, machines are collecting more and more data. As years progress, as decades progress, machines are getting swift and sleek in decision-making. Doesn't that scare the people who are building the future of work? Why will the organisation body that is building a future of work not be worried by the growth of machine learning and artificial intelligence? They have all the rights to be worried just like the astronomers of the 16th century who were looking at the planets and started using "naked eye". Every organisation has their right to opinion about usage of machine learning and artificial intelligence using data for future work, but not everyone will have their own facts. The future of work holistic design consideration has "data" as the "oil" on which the "engine" will run. But if the future of work is considered in isolation, the vision and data-centric model will not be clear. The data from humans, their environment, devices that they use, the network on which the data travels, and the applications that provide input and output of data collection activity will define the future of work.

Words of wisdom:

More the "data", merrier the "Future of work" is.

Your Future of work must capture, curate, and cultivate as much data as possible. These data will be collected from the environment where employee work, the devices they use, the network on which the data transmits, and last, but not the least, the application that operates on this data. Machines will help you to take your load off to make easy decisions based on these data correlations. You will have to keep taking the tough decisions.

18

DISTRIBUTED SYSTEMS

From:

Monolithic. It is humans who are mobile, not the devices (tools) that they use to get their work done. The nature of the work of humans inspires the system and tool designs. These designs make their work efficient and effective. In the late '40s, the first data centre of the world was built. In that era, the offices were monolithic and centralised. The designs of the offices were like a hub and spoke system model. For example, banks had branches and the branches used to send data to the head office. Schools had branches and each branch of the school was siloed in their information flow and access. Hence, the tool and work design evolved in a manner where the information was kept centrally and read-write of that information was done by workers using terminals. For example, retail point of sale machines would read-write sales data to a central location. The growth rate of business was directly proportional to the availability, scale, and resiliency of this central monolithic computer system and the number of terminals that could concurrently connect to it.

To:

Distributed. Exponential reduction in the cost of data network connectivity to the central location and multi-fold increase in strength of computing that is available in the hand of each human has challenged the old way of work and created new opportunities to create future of work. For example, in 1980, personal computers took only 100K orders by Christmas. Whereas, today, online distributed systems giants like Amazon can cater to 400K orders a day. Around 70% of the world's population is connected to the internet - ready to work. The workforce is distributed, the computers are distributed, and there is a network design that is capable in supporting the distributed system for future work. A distributed system will ensure that the compute capacity is elastic and will scale on-demand of business. A distributed system will allow the distributed workforce to connect and work based on the demand of the business. Distributed systems will bring resiliency to the organisations. Distributed systems will facilitate the following three models of business availability. For critical issues with a huge impact to the business, the whole system can be brought up within 30 minutes. With medium issues that impact a segment of the business, the system can be troubleshot and fixed within 8-10 hours. For low impact issues, the system can learn the issue and would like to pre-empt the resolution when the threshold of the issue reaches. The distributed workforce of the future of work will make the organisations more inclusive, attract talents from the globe, and allow the businesses to harness the potential of distributed technology and designs to grow the size of the pie instead of making a zero-sum model. The organisations that will allow a distributed workforce, use distributed computing, and keep distributed data will win the race of the future of work.

Words of wisdom:

"Future of work" is an opportunity to leverage distributed workforce, compute, and data.

The future of work has created the opportunity to leverage distributed workforce using distributed systems of technology. The challenge of monolithic systems design shall be strategically transformed with distributed systems design for existing organisations. For budding organisations, "distributed work" is the default design for future of work.

19

CUMBERSOME CODE

From:

Cumbersome and complex code. The closer the coding language is to the computer, more complex it is. The closer the coding language is to users, simpler it is. It is the trade-off between speed and scale that defines which type of coding language is apt for the work design. For example, the machine that goes to the moon needs to make decisions in seconds and needs to work on real-time operating systems for instant human-like decision-making. The investment of coding and programming "language" was done for mission-critical and high investment areas, like space research, banking, etc. In this era, while most of the world was writing and reading human language on paper, it used to require specific skills to write in a language that computers can understand. Because the language that computers can understand was complex, limited to specific hardware, and developer-intensive, the power of machine computation using coding was limited to certain areas and verticals of the industries. These limiting factors, a huge investment of time and money in developers, and the snail pace of creating code to do work are the challenges that the world is solving through the future of work.

To:

Simple and slick code. Wix, Minecraft, and Shopify are great examples of the new language learning platforms that are democratizing computer language skills. What the User Interface design of Windows did to personal computers containing Unix in the '80s, these digital applications creation platforms are doing the same for the coding language for future of work. Abstracting the coding language and complementing them with user experience and human-friendly designs will allow the digital systems become mainstream for the future of work. With this platform, a human with great design skills and a sense of logic will be able to create a platform on which their customers can buy their product - with "one-click". While this future of work developers will care about the emotive, empathetic, and experience aspect of the design of their website, the coding to invoke software programs on "one-click" will be abstracted and made available for them to use. The simple, slick, and swift coding language will take care of the complexity of inter-machine transactions. Gen Z, X, and Y are more comfortable in using their logical thinking to design and code their ideas on a digital platform, while the baby boomers and, up to an extent, millennials are still using physical white board and paper to create their design, and then, hiring a developer to translate their design and ideas in a way that is understandable by computers. The future of work language will reduce the time, effort, and money investment required to translate the idea of the human mind into a machine-readable language code. More the merrier - the more the number of humans who code, more will be the usage of the digital platforms for the future of work.

Words of wisdom:

"Future of work" will democratise "coding".

The future of work is making coding simple and swift for humans. It is possible because of abstraction of computer languages, evolution of human friendly digital designs, and comfort of upcoming generations with designs and computers. For example, Minecraft allows kids to create a computer game within hours, even though they don't know coding language, but are good with drawings with colours. Future of work is an opportunity for everyone to code.

20

ASSERTIVE AMBIENT

From:

Stationary. First-generation computers were stationary. They entered the human house in the form of a television, personal computer, or calculator. Irrespective of the form, they were stationary. Humans had to wake them up, very likely by pressing a button. Unless the button was pressed, they were physically present in the house but passive. Once they started, they used to do the task they were supposed to perform perfectly. And yes, they never use to talk to another computer in the home. For example, do you remember the first personal computer that came to your house in the 90s? They were powered on standby, connected to a universal power supply (UPS). Press a button, they will start, and the monitor will wake up. Give your commands and it will work for you. But the computer never talked to the TV in your house. Or even the telephone in your house. For the office too, the behaviour was equally the same, the computer never talked to the air conditioner or the door. So, when did machines started talking to each other? It was the remote of the television, the remote of the air conditioner, or the remote of the video cassette recorder, which showed the early signs that machines had started talking to the other. And the work they use to do was limited by the limited collaboration between the machines.

To:

Ambient. Computers are an integral part of work ambiance nowadays. They are assertive, active, and automatic, all at the same time. They are assertive because they can now tell you when to wake up, when to drink water, or when to take a break during your busy schedule. They have become active from passive. No more do you have to press a button to wake them up. They are always up, active, and doing their job. For example, the lighting in your office switches off automatically at 6.00 p.m. And in case anyone makes their presence felt by just a wave of the hand, they switch back on. So-called "mobile", the most powerful computer in your hand, talks and collaborates with most of the computers in your house and work. It talks to the air conditioner to set the right temperature. It talks to your laptop to seamlessly transfer the work browser as you walk into your desk. It opens the door of your car. It starts your scheduled meeting as soon as you enter the meeting room. This second generation of active computers will grow into the third generation of the future of work. The third generation computer of the future of work will be cognitive and importantly empathetic. The ambient computing power of humans will grow multi-fold as more and more sensors will start surrounding them in the future of work. The collaboration between these ambient sensors will allow the computers to become empathetic and cognitive to human needs. For the future of work, the technologists will consider social and behavioural design seriously. Is your future of work design-oriented towards building an empathetic ambiance?

Words of wisdom:

"Future of work" will keep "empathy" at the centre of design.

The future of work ambience will be built around empathy. The gap between human emotions and computer empathy will be more closely bridged. You must build applications using machine learning platforms so that they have empathy as core to their design principles. These designs will make your organisations and work environment ready for the next generation of workstyle.

21

MODERN MACHINES

From:

Contextual. Machines that help humans work are context-aware. They are aware of context because their capability to keep data with them has increased in conjunction with Moore's law. Their memory allows them to remember your location, the network connectivity options, the context of the device, and the pattern of work. They memorize these contexts of humans not for just hours or days, but months. Correlation of these contexts and time scale allows the machines to understand and predict the behaviour of human working style. As no two humans are the same genetically, their work style behaviour is not the same. Based on the understanding of individual behavioural workstyle, these machines recommend actions that help humans work better. For example, your phone can prompt you about an increase in travel time to the office when the weather is bad, just before your regular scheduled time when you leave for office. Another example is your watch, which can change the time automatically as soon as you come out of airplane mode after a 10-hour flight. Because your watch knows which timezone you have landed in, it changes the time in the calendar automatically for you and adjusts the time settings. These events are changing your behaviour, without you knowing it.

To:

Persuasive. The future of work machines will be persuasive. The more they know about you and your behaviour, the more persuasive they will be. The future of work will go beyond keeping your digital footprint to keeping your digital self. The more they know about the type of work that you do, the more they will try to make it easy for you. For example, imagine that your work is to market a product. And you need to hire a brand ambassador or advocate to enhance your product's brand image and impact. Today, it is almost impractical to measure the business impact and outreach of the prospect brand ambassador before signing him/her for your brand. You do your work based on quantitative data mixed with your expertise in the market. In the future of work, the machines will be able to proactively measure the impact or reach of the message given by an individual even before you sign them. You would able to choose the market segment, message type, and probable brand ambassador, and the machine will tell you the impact of the message that the respective individual can create for amplifying your product, proactively. This will help you to contract the right ambassador for the right segment and maximize the return on your investment of marketing budget. The confidence and accuracy of machines to persuade you will become better with time in the future of work.

Words of wisdom:

"Future of work" machine will be "persuasive".

The future of work machine will persuade your clients for desired outcomes. You will have to build or buy the awareness of digital avatar of your clients. The better the avatar of client is, better your machines will be able to persuade them. Immediately invest in persuasive technology, if not done yet, to increase the profitability of your future of work.

22

CONSISTENT CLOUD

From:

Product. Applications are built and run on three fundamentals pillars of technology infrastructure, namely network, computer, and storage. In the hay day of servers, one application used to run on one server. For example, one server used to run one operating system (mainly Unix or Windows). On top of that operating system, applications used to run. The tight coupling of one operating system to one hardware brought in the challenge of power consumption, space requirement, and on-demand scale. The "Virtualisation" of hardware solved this problem. Virtualization abstracted, pooled, and allocated resources to the application based on their requirement. This increased the availability and tolerance of the applications. More than two decades ago, organisations' IT teams started building their private cloud using the waterfall model. On these private clouds (namely datacentres) applications were built and run to cater to business demands. To build the cloud, the IT team procured hardware products. The procurement was a factor of the forecast of allocated budget to IT and demand of business to IT in the coming months. This product procurement, private cloud build, and scalable applications for business need cycles became a consistent, fundamental, and trustworthy model for successful businesses that used IT. The businesses started to demand more and fast from the private cloud.

To:

Services. Private clouds became agile when they became public around a decade ago. Often organisations use multiple infrastructure clouds now (mix of on-premise and public) to build their applications. Businesses are now demanding application service and service level agreement; they assume infrastructure is always available, on-demand. "Applications" became an integral and salient part of services that organisations offer to their customers a decade ago. Because of this focus and necessity to cater to client's needs, growth of context-aware applications started. The second generation of applications started to learn the location, device type, network type, screen resolution, and behaviour of the users so that they can offer more meaningful service to the users. For example, employees of any organisation need three services namely collaboration (e-mail), storage (to keep their data), and app store (like the first-generation desktop) to access their data. In the future of work, resiliency, continuity, and availability of these three services will increase. They will increase because the technologists will design these services on the infrastructure of multiple clouds. In future work, the mission-critical and highly sensitive applications of any organisation will run on their private cloud and on-demand variable service workload application will run on the public cloud. For example, one keeps their money in the bank, but their precious gems or stones in a safe, which is more reliable, secure, and trustworthy. Future work will balance out the trade-off of cloud services to make them consistent. Customer demands from applications will drive this consistency of the cloud for the future of work.

Words of wisdom:

"Future of work" cloud will deliver consistent "application services".

The future of work will make the cloud consistent and mature for consumption. Organisations will invest in reliability, availability, and consistency of application services. This investment will complement the "consistent cloud" design of organisation of future of work. You must create a blueprint of cloud platform to build and run future of work application services.

23

EMOTION ENVIRONMENT

From:

Behaviour. Applications are learning and observing your behaviour. They are doing this so that they can increase the profitability of organisations, compete better against other applications, and provide data insights to business owners to create the right product for their consumers. For example, imagine you are planning a Christmas vacation with your family to Hawaii in June. As part of your initial research, on a weekend, you do a basic search and query so that you can discuss and plan your itinerary within the respective budget. Following that weekend, you might observe that, very likely, your social media platforms will start prompting you with advertisements related to travel to Hawaii. The prompts appear very timely and very often. This is an example of behavioural learning and response by a prompt. "Behaviour Data" and "Application" to process that data are two Lego blocks that join together to shape the desired outcome. While the data capture is limited by the cost of data and network, the crunching of this data is limited by the platform on which the applications are written.

With time, the cost of keeping data and networks is coming down exponentially. The applications are more and more built on an "artificial intelligence" platform instead of an infrastructure cloud platform. This era is the cusp of the future of work application. The measure of emotions of humans doesn't have a metric but is like a continuum. This continuum depends on a lot on measurable environmental factors. The correlation of observation of these environmental factors to the emotions of humans is what the future applications will make possible.

To:

Persuasion. Future of work applications are persuasive. They are persuasive because they use are built on machine learning models. These models help them learn every minute, hour, and day. These applications are also persuasive because they have access to a plethora of data points about one human. For example, the future of work applications will be able to measure the carbon footprint of an individual. Based on these measurements, the application will persuade users for "small steps" so that their digital footprint measurement gets better. Concepts powered by capabilities to persuade will create a future of work. These capabilities are ensuring that an application engages more with the user by understanding their emotions rather than just the context of behaviour. *"Persuasion happens to be more of an art than science"* - a wise man said once. And the art of building application starts when the technologists design the application. The design phase of the future of work applications must take the "social" and "behavioural" aspect of emotions of the users of applications. An excellent design generates future of work application. Often during the design phase, the emotions of the users are not missed out. Future of work application design will be emotion-inclusive. This will require experts of human emotion understanding, like HR professionals or social science experts, to be involved during the design phase. The role of data scientists will also be critical during this phase. They are the ones who will be able to understand the requirement of a "confidence score" of emotional calculations. The translation of design to a tangible application will require continuous running of the applications on an agile and self-healing basis. Just like practice makes a man perfect, iteration will make persuasion perfect for the future of work applications. How are you investing in understanding the emotions of your employees? Survey?

Words of wisdom:

Applications of "Future of work" are "emotive and persuasive".

The future of work applications will engage more with emotions of the users. Such applications will be built on machine learning platform. They will understand the emotions of humans better. The understanding of emotions will be used to engage with humans better. You must design applications taking social and behavioural context of employees into account for future of work.

24

SERVER TO SERVER-LESS

From:

Servers were the foundational element of enterprise applications half a century ago. Just like the nucleus is the centre of the atom, the server was the nucleus of the datacentre. There were small, medium, large and extra-large servers. Servers design and computing power drove the nature and potential of the application performance. The digital work outcome of an organisation was directly proportional to the number of servers running in their datacentre. While they grew linearly in the early years, the growth became exponential around the late 90s. "Server" design depended upon many critical but crucial components. To give you a perspective, a server's power to perform depends on the resonance of the components like processor, BIOS (basic input/output system), motherboard chipset, memory cards, PCIe bus, network adaptor, storage adaptor, and operating system. You must be thinking it would take a village to build a server, and that was true. As you can observe, the interoperability of all these components was a painful task. An organisation's technology leaders spent a significant cycle of their work to discuss, design, procure, build, and interoperate the datacentre elements. The beauty was that the datacentres were owned by the organisations, like a prized possession. And because of the value they brought in, there was consistent demand to grow them, at lesser cost and in less time. A good challenge to have.

To:

Service. Less is more. The serverless framework gives just an Application Programmable Interface service to the organisation. The organisation doesn't have to invest time and infrastructure in procuring, keeping, and running hardware resources. For example, just like you order an Uber, instead of keeping a car in your garage. The agility provided by the serverless framework has transformed the waterfall application design into the agile design. In a serverless framework, the cloud provider dynamically manages the allocation of machine resources. In the wake of this advancement, the organisations pay the cloud based on the number of machine resources consumed by the applications, instead of a pre-purchased unit of machine capacity. Auto-scaling, resiliency, elasticity, availability, and service level agreement takes precedence in a serverless framework. The line of business will increase investment in a serverless framework to the drive the digital footprint and growth in future of work. The future of work application design will focus on the services instead of the server. The quality of the service and its impact on business will be discussed and evaluated in the future of work. The consistency of this API service built on a serverless framework will build trust between organisations and cloud providers. For the future of work applications, organisations will not like to lock-in with one cloud vendor. Instead, organisations will adopt a platform design approach that will allow the applications to run and migrate to serverless vendors giving the most value, including on-premise cloud.

Words of wisdom:

Applications of "Future of work" MUST be agile and available.

The future of work application will be agile and available. They will have these capabilities as they will be built on serverless framework offered by cloud providers. While your organisation will pay for the resource consumed by applications, the cloud providers will own the quality of service. For mission critical applications, organisations will build their private serverless framework.

25

SECURITY SCENARIO

From:

Speed breaker. Imagine you made a 100-km long highway. Your highway infrastructure is also capable of allowing cars to run at their maximum potential speed. The governance body told you to ensure that nearly no-accident should happen on your highway. Then, what will you do? You could use speed breakers, speed limiting signboards, and penalties for non-compliance. Very similar is the story of infrastructure security build-out. Whenever the stretch of highway was built in the organisation, the security was bolted on for that patch of stretch. For example, when servers were bought, server security products were purchased. When network elements were bought and built, network security elements were purchased. When applications were built, application security elements on servers, storage, and networks were purchased. This created multiple speed breakers in the performance flow of work in the organisation. Not only was the security limited to allow access to the full potential of infrastructure, the compliance was also reactive. For example, if the incident occurred, the penalty would have been levied.

Usually, if the benefit from breaking the compliance rule is significantly higher than the cost of the penalty, the security compliance is broken.

To:

Frictionless. Future of work security framework will be frictionless. It will be frictionless because it will be based on the pro-active behaviour analysis principles, instead of reactive piecemeal speed breaker designs. It will be frictionless because it will be able to authenticate users based on their biological characteristics, like the retina, palm-vein, heart-beat, and voice, instead of a monolithic password or a combination of the machine-generated keys. For example, palm vein-based authentication for a bank's ATM user is already in use in Japan for almost half a decade. Amazon ONE is another example of a future of work-centric frictionless security framework-based application access. A wise man once said, *"Everyone has the right to have their own opinion, but not their own facts"*.As the organisations will adopt a serverless API-centric platform approach, they will also adopt a shared risk-based framework with the cloud providers. This framework will also help the organisations break the silos of data-centre security, network security, and end-user security. Once the silos will be broken in the future of work design, the framework will capture the data continuously from multiple touchpoints. Based on these captured data-points and their co-relation, the future of work security framework will be able to proactively identify and segregate the bad behaviours from the unusual behaviour. And the automation will kick-in to either quarantine, resolve, or restart the whole system to ensure that the surface of attack is reduced and minimalized by bad behaviour identification.

Words of wisdom:

Applications of "Future of work" MUST be fact driven.

The future of work applications will be driven by facts. As fact changes, the application behaviour will also change. For example, the fact like abnormal user location change will stop the application access to the user.

26

GROWING G
(3-4-5 AND BEYOND)

From:

Zero G. It is not technology that is mobile, it is human. Mobile technology, on its own, doesn't have value unless it solves the problem of mobile human. The problem of "work while mobile" was first solved DIGITALLY with the advent of *second generation* mobile phones in 1991. This mobile phone standard was built on TDMA (Time Division Multiple Access) and FDMA (Frequency Division Multiple Access) encoding methods. Do you wonder how mobile human was identified by the network in 1991? By the invention of subscriber identity module (SIM) card. SIM card didn't solve the problem of bandwidth availability, but it did resolve mobile human identification. O.1 Mb its per second was the maximum download speed available with GPRS 2G. Mobile humans primarily need three types of information to work, namely voice (to talk), video (to see), and data (to inform). Today a 4G LTE network provides a download bandwidth of 90Mbits per second, an increase of approximately

900,000% compared to the download bandwidth capability in 1991. Not only can you imagine, but today, you experience the benefit of a humongous increase in bandwidth every day. How? By observing. Observe the video pixel quality (4K/8K) that you see on YouTube. Observe the size of the file, photo, or video that you share as an email attachment. Observe the soothing sound quality of your mobile voice call. Observe that song download today takes 3seconds, which would have otherwise taken 7 minutes in the 2G era. Today, 4G technology is not just delivering the value of WORK, but the value of EXPERIENCE. And this is just the beginning of #Futureofwork.

To:

Five G. Imagine around 900% increase in the maximum download speed of what you use today. That's the #Futureofwork mobile network available to you– with 5G. Voice, video, and data slices of the mobile network will become more efficient and capable of solving a business use case. Future of work network will allow create a slice in the network, for example, aslice of IOT device network, a slice of smart cars communication, a slice of broadband communication, etc. With this network, every industry will transform in the way they work today. For example, the automobile industry will have the "internet of cars" that will allow smart cars to talk to each other on their allocated network slice. The education industry vertical will stream artificial reality and virtual reality images on AR/VR network slice. In the healthcare industry, a doctor will do critical and crucial surgery remotely, on their safe and secure network slice. "Vehicle to everything" (V2X) will allow governance and policing information to be shared, with resiliency, on their dedicated network slice. As you can see, across the industries, these changes will not just be transformative, but disruptive. These changes will be based on future of work design directly mapped to the requirement of business use case. If designed well, the future of work with 5G will be able to deliver EXPERIENCE beyond expectations.

Words of wisdom:

"Future of work" with 5G design must be mapped to business use case.

The future of work network technology will go beyond mere voice, video, and data slices. They will allow you to create custom network slices mapped to your business use case objects. You must take a "wholistic" approach to design inputs and outputs of #Futureofwork network, instead of silos.

27

QUANTUM QUEST

From:

Finite. Semiconductor innovation was a "finite" revolution. It disrupted the analog world by converting it into a binary world. Human kind started translating, operating, and storing everything in form of bits, that is, as 0 and 1. Any wave generated in the world, like voice, light, etc., got translated into 0 and 1. After this first step of translation, basic finite logical operations, like addition and subtraction,were performed on that binary data. The generated binary or sequence of binary output is kept and displayed as required. Look around yourself and you will, very likely, find that you are surrounded by binary digital displays – the screen on which you are reading this book, the smart watch that is resting on your wrist, the stock market quotes displayed on screen,and even the autonomous cars on the road. The financial industry was the first one to leverage binary systems for the benefit of transforming work. Handwritten details of financial transactions were translated from physical paper books to digital binary registers. The financial calculations on such binary information advanced rapidly. Storing financial information became both weather- and time-proof. Using binary information empowered trade at higher frequency via complex algorithms. It was 1959, when Bank of America first used computers to automate book-keeping. Since then, the work of financial calculation transformed into optimization problems. The bank's traders, assisted by models running on classical computers, worked to generate returns of the order of 19-20%. The gain return on work is directly proportional to the hardware and software program. Both of which are *finite* in nature.

To:

Infinite. Algorithmic calculation is not limited by software, it is limited by hardware. The finite limit of classical computers are slowing down the algorithmic models, slowing down the dollar per instruction, and slowing down the machine's power to make decisions. The very near term resolution of this hardware limitation is *"Quantum Computing"*. In 1980, physicists envisioned that the counter-intuitive properties of quantum mechanics might allow for building of computers that could attain mathematical feats that no non-quantum machine would ever be capable of. Analogous to "bits" of classical computers, "qbits" are the measure of stability of quantum computers. Quantum computers, with thousands of stable qbits,are undoubtedly much faster than any non-quantum machine in solving many large and complex problems of #Futureofwork. Though, such machines don't yet exist. What exist today are unstable devices that can perform calculations only for tiny fractions of a second before their delicate quantum state breaks down. John Preskill of California Institute of Technology calls this as "NISQs - Noisy, Intermediate-Scale Quantum Computer". In

2019, Google demonstrated the first quantum supremacy using 53-qbit NISQs. It performed calculations within a minute that would have otherwise taken more than 10,000 years for the world's fastest classical computer to do. Imagine the infinite power of hardware in a decade. Vendors reckon that 1000-qbit machines will be built by 2023. Leading industry vendors have talked about the availability of millions of qbits by the end of the decade. In the short term, credit scoring will very likely be a plausible application to revolutionize the future of work for the finance industry. Healthcare, manufacturing, and space research industries will exponentially be benefitted by the qb its computing capability like "digital twins". Your future of work's dollar per instruction has the capability to grow multi-fold with the realisation of quantum quest of humans.

Words of wisdom:

"Future of work" will have billions times more computing capability powered by qbits.

The complex and critical future of work algorithms will run on quantum computers. With stabilization of qbits, quantum applications will grow, imparting enhanced profitability and agility to business. Computers will not only run complex computational models, and will do so with agility. As #Futureofwork will provide the hardware quantum leap to every industry, your head-start with quantum ready software model will put you in a leader's position.

28

SIMPLE SOFTWARE

From:

Low Code. Machine level, assembly level, and high level are three levels in which software is written. Software is not complex, software level is complex. Closer the level of software to the machine, higher the complexity of work and expertise required to write the software. As you can see, there was a need for harmonious and mutually integral software development across the levels. *"Waterfall model"* proved to be a stable, high-quality, and time-tested enterprise grade software. As the name suggests, the flow was sequential across levels, each level had high quality requirements, and the next level had a high degree of interdependence on the previous level. The trade-off between time taken and quality was one of the challenges that organisations solved in this era by organising their release upgrade cycle. For example, the hardware will refresh typically in a three-year cycle. This hardware upgrade cycle is used to ensure that the latest time tested machine and assembly level software are ready for the next three years. This upgrade was followed byhigh-level software upgrade. This lifecycle for each organisation was time-consuming, slow, labour-intensive and, more importantly, non-agile. Moreover, as you know, the demand of business from IT kept increasing exponentially, putting a breakpoint where things have to be pivoted to support #Futureofwork needs from software.

To:

No Code. Less is more - future of work software dilemma has this principal ingrained in organisations. The less hardware they manage, the more they can scale. The less software they build and manage themselves, the more **agile** their future of work model will be. This has created a spectrum amongst organisations. On one side are the modern future-ready organisations that barely keep anything inside their organisation and leverage on-demand teams, resources, and applications to get their outcomes delivered. Fintechs, online learning platforms, like schools, growing start-up ecosystems, non-profitable organisations, digital personal businesses, are few examples of these types of organisations. Platforms like Wix, Shopify, etc. are great examples that cater to the demand of these agile organisations. In this world, a business' software can be built for #Futureofwork in a matter of hours. On the other side of the spectrum, there are organisations like financial institutions that have a huge footprint of monolithic, waterfall-based software systems. These organisations are transforming on the fly, ensuring that their flight is intact with business running as usual. Outside these two spectrums, there is a leading indicator. Within this indicator, the humans workers are not writing software at all. They get the machine bootstrapped to a level where it can understand the problem, learn the solution, and create the model itself to respond to the problem.

For example, you remember the autonomous floor cleaner in your house, or the pilot of an autonomous car, in which millions of lines of codes are burnt at once, but they respond to the day to day solution needsontheir own. These models of low to no code will transform the workstyle for the betterment of humans. I was very glad to see the ongoing pilot of "autonomus garbage collector" truck in Singapore, a #smart nation. The low and no code future of work will attract human talent to drive higher order creative thinking job, which they like to do. The power to do more with less work of higher quality will be imparted by software as a foundation in #Futureofwork. Are you doing any #smartwork in your organisation?

Words of wisdom:

"Future of work" software will drive bigger machines, with less software.

The future of work hardware to software ratio will increase exponentially. While the size of hardware controlled by software will grow multi-fold, the size of software will decrease relatively. Software will be agile, high-quality, resilient, and scalable. You should try to leverage this strong integration to create higher order and smart #Futureofwork for your organisation.

29

PROTOTYPE PRODUCTION

From:

Product. Pre #Futureofwork, if i may say, customers used to buy FINISHED PRODUCTS. The customer evaluated products only after they were shipped and had gone through a step by step creation cycle. Products that were validated and tested for quality. The cycle of conceptualization, design, build, and finish is owned by the organisations. The cycle of buy, try, and deploy at scale was owned by customers. Any issues post-deployment, if found, would go as feedback to the organisation that built the product. The iteration would then happen again before a new version of the product was released. This was a long and slow iterative cycle. Intermediate agents between product manufacturing companies and end consumers further added to this delay. With time, it was observed that products depending upon hardware are slow, products depending upon software are fast. With this observation and realisation, the production and work of most of the industry shifted towards software. It shifted to software to solve the problem of slow service shipment to clients, longer innovation cycle, and increased competitiveness in the industry. Automobile industry is a great example here. During the industrial era, a car used to be built in factories, and then,sent to the dealers for demo and sale. Clients used to buy that car from dealers and report back in case there were any issues. As most of the components of a car were hardware, the lead cycle to fix the problem used to involve a change in the production cycle of the companies. This model is disrupted now, isn't it? But why?

To:

Prototype. Invention is not PRODUCTION. Innovation is PRODUCTION. With the amount of patents not fructifying as products, the world has realised that the best way to build products is by listening and catering to clients' needs, wants, and requirements. Instead of building a product and then taking to the client, #Futureofwork will involving the building of products other way around. This whole process will be agile, creative,collaborative, and co-innovative. Imagine that you can share an idea with the world as a minimum viable product (MVP), as the first stage. Then, gather the feedback on whether the need and the requirement of the client match your design. Then, deliver the product that caters to most of the needs of the clients. And iterate on this cycle of product building and innovation. Soon, once your organisation has a small client base, the other clients will come to know of the existence of your products, so they will also start collaborating with your organisation to buy the product. Often, most of the clients, nations, or geographies accept the product with the existing feature;however, this way of co-innovation to build the product allows broader adoption of the product for specific needs. Instead of articulation, selling, and product demonstration, the skills like empathy, design, and experience will harbour more importance for client-centric work of #Futureofwork. In order to rotate faster between the product delivery and feedback cycle, the organisations would see the middle agents becoming co-collaborators. As the needs of the organisations are slightly different, the product of the future of work should fulfil as much of the needs of the organisation as possible for broader adoption. Software-driven product and business models will gain the benefits of this model at a faster rate in future of work as they will be able to innovate at a super-fast pace. Let's look at the example of automobile industry. While a few years back, barely a few thousands lines of software were used as part of the car product, now a days, a car can have as high as tens of millions lines of coderunning on them. Future of work will require co-innovation and collaboration to build products that are more meaningful for your clients, especially leveraging software.

Words of wisdom:

"Future of work" will have more INNOVATION than INVENTION.

The future of work will keep "empathy" at the centre of design. Clients will co-innovate and involve early in the product development cycle that will reduce the time of product development and increase the quality. Collaboration, Inclusion, and Prototyping will increase to leverage the growth opportunity of #Futureofwork. You MUST create an environment of critical feedback loop with clients to ensure product success in #Futureofwork.

PART FIVE

STRATEGY

30

EXQUISITE EXPERIENCE

From:

Performance. *Performance* and *quality* were two pillars of success strategy in the industrial era. The quality of inventory, workforce, and output of organisation was the determining factor of the success of organisation longevity. The performance of workers or machines producing the product of the organisation was in direct correlation to the quality expectation. The western world devised many ways to improve *performance*, while the eastern world focused on *quality*. If you think deeply, you will realize that each of them were important to two different entities in the horizontal product consumption chain. Performance was important for organisation. Quality was important for the customer. A wise man once said, *"Quality is well remembered after the price is forgotten"*. And to benchmark and bring credibility to a product, several institutions were created to certify the quality of the product. The quality certificate was a good measure to satisfy clients. The scope and credibility of the quality certificate or qualifying organisation was limited by geographical boundaries put by the communication medium.

Why? Because of absence of the internet. For example, cars made in the western world were meeting the quality benchmark of the west, and eastern world products met the benchmark of the east. Isn't it strange that the humans were the same, but their quality benchmarks were different. The advent of the internet was a breakthrough. The humans all around the world got the power and the platform to access the same information on "earth", anywhere. Their *experience* changed.

To:

Experience. *"People don't remember what you said. People always remember how they felt"*.These people are the workers of #Futureofwork. Future of work employees are not just experiencing, but are expressing too. They are expressing themselves NOT in the enterprise world, but in the consumer world. The consumer experience of senders in the social network is influencing the consumer experience of the receivers quite often. *"Network Effect"*is the emerging strategy for creating and capturing value in the future of work. TikTok, Wechat, WhatsApp, etc. are great examples of the organisations that are creating and capturing value of *network effect*. Collaboration is complementing the future of work strategy, humongously. Collaboration is creating community-community of employees and customers who are praising, believing, and aligning to organisation purpose. For example, a future of work automobile manufacturer who believes that automobiles should run on clean technology, like electric or solar, will have a humongous community of clients and employees supporting him. The impact of influencing the future of work employees with network effect can be so meaningful that the highly qualified and skilful workers might work for your organisation at a cheaper salary. Numerous mushrooming unicorns are testimony of the fact that the employees are working in companies for their belief and their experience. Authenticity and sanctity of the experience is touching human hearts, not just minds. To stay relevant and become successful, the leading and pioneering organisations of the future of work are giving a delightful, meaningful, and purposeful experience to their employees, not just clients. The organisations of the future of work have well-defined and communicated strategy of building products to save earth (sustainability), humanity, and equality (inclusion). Is your organisation delivering an exquisite and exclusive experience?

Words of wisdom:

"Future of work" strategy MUST have/include "Experience" at the core.

Future of work strategy will be experience-driven. Experience of employees and clients of an organisation will define the longevity and profitability of the organisation. Nurturing natural experience of humans will make your organisation love able. The business, IT, and HR strategies must inculcate and internalize your organisation's "Experience" strategy.

31

JOVIAL JOBS

From:

Jobs. Industrial revolution created jobs. Jobs were tasks that humans did for consistent and homogeneous output. Human input skill, when applied to do a task, generated output. This is the principle applied to jobs. Mundane and monotonous in nature, jobs are predictable and deliver predictable outputs. For example, an individual collecting money at the teller of a bank or an individual sitting at a counter issuing train tickets. Organisations, during the industrial revolution, mastered this art to scale and become predictable in their output. *Fixed mindset* is the human behaviour that is well-suited for these kinds of work. The change in skill is catered by planned training. The human, at a particular level of skill, is given training to step up their skill to do better tasks. For example, the train ticket issuer or the bank teller is trained to use computers to do the same task, quickly and more efficiently. As you see, the job stays the same, humans stay the same, the skill upgrade can be planned. Based on the skill upgrade, the output profit as well as the profitability of the organisation can be planned. At the same time, with increase in the critical thinking ability of the machines, the tasks that were predictable and measurable could be offloaded to machines. For example, ATMs can do the job of human tellers, ticketing machines can do the job of the ticket issuer. Organisations always had to make a decision regarding the trade-off between keeping people and using optimised machines to do the job. Why might this have happened? Because the said job doesn't use critical thinking and holistic personality of humans. The time of this job transition from human to machine of 20 years was a good period. This cycle of job transfer has reduced significantly. In fact, in a lot of cases it has shortened to 2-5 years. Future of work is accelerated and is evident.

To:

Career. *PURPOSE is MORE POWERFUL than POWER itself.* Whole is greater than the sum of its parts. Imagine when the future of work employees will bring their whole self to the purpose of your organisation instead of a partial self for doing a task. Their creativity, contribution, and value captured by the organisation will be priceless and limitless. With the proliferation of **remote work first** and **distributed workforce** strategies, the workers will focus on career, not jobs. They might have more than one career over the period of week. These two careers will be well-balanced and, ideally, non-conflicting. For example, a developer may also be a music teacher, or a public speaking coach may also be an insurance broker. The infusion of the learning and the skills to mutually benefit the optimized and time-bound goals will be the new norm in the future of work. "More with less", both the organisations and the workers of the future of work will demonstrate that. The shift of the general mindset from fixed to growth will be a transformational shift that will be instrumental is driving these behaviours in the future of work. Fixed mindset workers are great at doing the same thing again and again, comfortably and willingly. They soon stop using their heart and mind to do that job. On the other hand, a career is something where an employee wants to evolve for betterment of both, organisation and oneself. And the answer to evolution is a mindset of growth, i.e. growth mindset. As the client's needs are changing and evolving at a pace faster than ever before in history, the strategy to build a growth mindset is the right strategy. In the future of work, the career will be built by accepting challenges, overcoming obstacles, persevering in face of scarcity, consistent critical feedback, and learning from history. A strategy to change the mindset of the organisation is the right one to get on the path of success, if not already done so.

Words of wisdom:

"Future of work" employees will choose career over jobs, more often.

Future of work employees will bring their individualism to work, more than today. The mindset of continuous meaningful learning will create careers for employees. The organisations of future of work MUST provide the learning platform to transform the behaviour of employee, quickly.

32

INCLUSIVE INTENT

From:

Exclusive. *"Walk the talk"* is not easy. "Walk the talk" is Hard. The "exclusive" institutions and organisations often depict the ratio of nationality, gender, and race in their reports. While their strategy is to communicate that they are *exclusive*, the outcome doesn't correlate. For example, imagine you are looking for the best swimming club. Will you be choosing an exclusive swimming club that published the list of timings of swimming (i.e. swimming performance)? Or instead, you will choose a club that published the list of the gender, nationality, and race ratio of their members? The intent of exclusivity limits itself till the infusion of power and pride. The **exclusive** organisations can be unique, but they might not be the best. Their exclusivity is oriented towards creating a "brand perception". And you know what happens to a brand if it's not authentic, credible, and emotionally engaging to the people. For example, there are numerous stories of college dropouts who became more successful than the "exclusive" students who pursued "education" in the college. If you think about why, there could be two reasons:

One, the students got influenced by the "exclusivity" report. Two, someone else took their decisions on their behalf. The one who dropped out were more individualistic and objective about their intent and goals. As the future of work is infusing the upcoming, decisive, opinionated, and individualistic new generations, the value of "exclusivity" is often challenged.

To:

Inclusive. Future of work will be very analogous to an Olympic game. There will be many types of gaming competitions: individuals, groups, and teams. And for each of the games, the players are the best at that particular sport. The teams for a sport will be formed quickly, will have apt skill, and will deliver an outcome in short time duration. And that too, again and again. For example, if you form a team to swim 800m, let the four swimmers swim 200m each. Why invite someone to a swimming team, if he is a good runner, and more importantly, wants to run? An *"inclusive"* organisation of the future of work will be built on credibility, authenticity, and passion to deliver. With remote work gaining momentum, you can't expect to create a school of training where you bring all the employees in a room, train them on how to sell autonomous vehicles, and send them to sell autonomous cars. Instead, future of work employees will most likely be passionate about autonomous cars. Since they will be passionate about autonomous cars, they will find themselves amongst the group of passionate community members. They will also go to libraries, on social media, and the internet to enhance their skills and awareness about day to day happenings in the area of autonomous cars. They will give feedback, mostly critical about what is moving and needs to be moved to stay relevant. They will expect a response on guidance on what needs to be communicated to the clients, inclusively. The future of work inclusive community will be physically apart, but the future of work *inclusive community will be globally virtually knit*. **The community will play bigger and more important role than committees.** For example: cryptocurrency. The *chief inclusive officer* strategy for future of work should be to provide clarity, be incharge of the inclusive community, and help the community, inclusively.

Words of wisdom:

"Future of work" organisation will not be exclusive, it will be inclusive.

Future of work organisation strategy will often not build on opinion, but on fact. The fact gathered from historic points will allow the strategy to connect the dots in the future. The inclusive team will be the one that will be meaningful and not exclusive.

33

GLOBAL GESTURE

From:

Language Limit. Languages are of two types, half and full. Half language communicates the numeric and logical message. Full language expresses emotions and feelings as part of a message. With the advent of globalisation, English became the primary language of conversation. Remember *business communications guide?* While the half language travels the globe without any hurdles, the full language loses its *essence in translation.* Technology has been trying hard to fill the gap of *"lost in translation"*. You know what I am saying if you have used the translator function of your browser to translate the language of a webpage. It has not been successful to a large extent because translation loses the emotion, translation loses the culture, and translation loses the empathy. Additionally, the consistent push to the society to become perfect in English has also not helped the non-English nations and speakers. There are nations where the languages or words are read in different order. You can imagine how hard it is to translate the order of the message to comprehend it. Voltaire once said, *"Don't allow the perfect to* *be the enemy of good."* While an intelligent human knows the words that he needs, the practicality is that he may not have them all ready for active service. So, how can an organisation of the future not get limited by the use of language?

To:

Expressing ideas. *If a picture is worth a thousand words, an emoji is worth millions. Isn't it?* Haven't you used *stickers* to express yourself? Aren't your friends sending you *gifs* to praise you on your success? Which one is easier - or a 30-word sentence in English stating what is it? The internet, email, and texting conversation has given birth to a new language, which apparently is better in expressing ideas, instead of just words. Mies Van Der Rohe had principled *"Less is more"*. He showed that the function and beauty of every object could be highlighted through the omission of certain elements. By removing the unnecessary words, the global communication gesture of future of work has helped humans express their ideas quickly, effectively, and globally. The language of the majority is often not formal, but casual. Then, why would you think that the future of work language of expressing ideas will be *formal and time taking*? Moreover, there is no school or business communication class that teaches how to use emojis or gifs. The organisations, employees, and clients of future of work are comfortable in bringing in their consumer life learning their office or their buying decisions. The largest and the biggest online shops have an icon of or expressing whether the product is good or not? The ratio of good to bad can be well-reported and read by consumers now instead of lengthy non-understandable quality reports of a product. Well, how many times do you read a *privacy policy* of a website or an organisation?

Words of wisdom:

"Future of work" people will not just use words. Future of work people will use gestures, global gestures.

Future of work employees and clients will use casual mode of gesture and communication. The evolving mode of internet language will remove the boundary and limit of legacy language. For broader and global outreach and cross communication, future of work organisations should use tools that support creating, building, and using internet language.

34

GREEN GOAL

From:

Confident that we are green. Nature is forever putting a premium on reality. Humans received the pristine, real and green earth. In the capitalist world, the *Green* solution didn't make sense. The priority to make profit ignored the nature. And over a period of time, nature's degradation became bigger than not just profit, but all the problems. The assumption that the earth is green, rather, will stay green, was proven a myth. *Economics doesn't know its debt to nature.* The developing economies played with dirty rules for half a century in the interest of profitability. And the rules changed when the problem was realized. The emerging and evolving economies of the world are not adapting to play with the new rule. Sustainable sourcing of raw materials, responsible emission during production, and waste disposal with integrity requires functional and foundation change in policy and production line. The momentum to be sustainable is so strong that the visionaries have already taken steps starting a few years ago. They are funding businesses that benefit from natural calamities, like building and designing walls on rivers, replacing cement with glass in the infrastructure design, etc. *Sustainability index* of organisations is a big leap in the history of humankind. The change to become sustainable is a huge cost to companies and consumers alike. The *Green* switch to products and services, like public transport, electricity, or consumer goods, comes with a significant price of lost time and quality to consumers in most places. And sustainable products, like vehicles, are still priced beyond the range of most existing budgets. Eco-friendly consumer goods and organic products are hard to find in score. Becoming sustainable for better tomorrow is not about confidence, but about conviction to create a green future of work.

To:

Convicted that we will be green. Humans are influenced by their environments. *"The less there is for you, the more is the need for you to make the most of what there is for you,"* a wise man once said. Analysing the cause of sustainability issues spectrum requires that bigger challenges should be handled first and with priority. Analysis suggests that 40% of the emission challenges come from the electricity generation. Non-renewable coal replacement with renewable sources of electricity will make the conviction a reality. Remaining 60% of the emission problem arises from other sectors, like transportation, industries, building, and others. The net zero sustainable future of work goals require two models. One, to transform the *existing* model towards becoming sustainable. The existing business model will have to be modelled in the future of work around recycling and reuse. For example, the waste collectors in Solapur, India, convert food waste into biogas for additional revenue. Second, to build new infrastructure and transport systems that are sustainable right from the day they are conceived. This will also need commercialization of the inventions by innovation. This horizontal integration of the value chain is creating jobs and making the investors profitable. Agriculture, for example, uses technology to turn their emission into useful carbon for vertical integration into the system. The cost of solar photovoltaic cell-generated power has reduced by 82% in the last decade. This has created the fastest growing and blue collar industry for growth. Value creation and capturing for the known renewable source of energy, like wind and solar, provides huge opportunities and challenges for your future of work. Which of these two buckets your organisation is in?

Words of wisdom:

"Future of work" is green.

The more "green" your strategy is, the more profitable your future of work will be. Every minute effort to become green will reap in magnitude of benefits to your organistaion in mid to long term.

35

MONDAY MOTIVATION

From: ■

Thank god, it's Friday. An expression of gratitude that work week is almost over. The weekend,filled with non-work activities, will start soon. In 1978, a movie was named with the same name. It was about disco culture. This culture lifestyle and motivation depicts "containerisation". One container of five-day (8 hours each day) work week, and another of two-daynon-work week. And yes, this culture of boxes also brings toppings of "paid leaves" - a magical privilege to reduce your work container sometimes. Most likely and often these magic privileges are not utilized by employees who are really passionate and motivated for the purpose of organisation. I think this is a universal truth and 80:20 rule can be applied to this fact. Let's take a look at life in this era. A customer can't take out money from the bank because it's the weekend. A student can't learn during the weekend because the library is closed. A consumer can't buy groceries on weekends because the shop is closed. Your electronics good or network connection can't be fixed if it's a weekend. Often these were work styles and cultures of the disco era. The future of work, or rather, workspace, has blurred the boundaries of the containers. These lines have blurred as the services offered by organisations have evolved. If there is anything today that you are okay with not getting seven days a week, it is most likely a "non-essential" in your life. Same stands true for what your organisation is or will deliver to your consumers in the future of work.

To:

#Monday Motivation. Its 2021. Distributed workspace, empathetic organisations, and passion-driven employees are a reality. Future of work has created the culture to empower purpose. Honestly, if machines can be autonomous, there is no reason that humans can't be. Future of work employees are not bound by time, they are liberated by freedom. Freedom to work when they want, where they want, and how they want. They shop anytime, they read anytime, their bank is open 24×7. Future of work organisations are allowing employees to manage their work and leisure time with themselves, their peers, and their families. The boundaries of containers are infused between work and life. The more the work is part of structured life, the more comfortable and energised are the employees. The more purpose-driven they are, the more motivated they are. Often the employees are thinking and are aware of who they are without the brand of their employer. They are speakers, influencers, problem solvers, writers, and team players. And that's the reason future of work organisations have stopped periodic performance review. The organisations of future of work have started employing people not on basis of degree but how skilled they are for the task. Most likely, the traditional education system would need to pace up to match with the motivation of the upcoming future of work.

Words of wisdom:

"Future of work" strategy will not be time-bound, future of work strategy MUST be purpose-bound.

Future of work organisations will trust and liberate employees MORE. The freedom to work anytime, the freedom to work anywhere, the freedom to take leave responsibly will drive the motivation-based culture. The employees of future of work not just work 8 hours for 5 days, they work for 40 hours spread throughout the week. Your organisation should build strategy to support this culture to drive motivation for future of work.

36

PURPOSE PRINT

From:

Subtraction. Michelangelo's strategy is based on subtraction strategy. *"I saw the angel in the marble and carved it until I set him free,"* he said. In this strategy, once the idea is conceptualized, layers of marbles are reduced to make the idea a reality. A huge piece of marble is taken, and then, carved layer by layer, shape by shape, over a period of time, to build the product. At the end, on one side, you have the finished product, and on the other, the waste that is generated while carving out the marble. Imagine if one carves the tree, the produced waste takes years to replenish. Often the manufacturing, transportation, infrastructure, or education industries are hugely impacted by this design principle. For example, before they start carving the marble, or in their case, iron or cement, they have to source them. This horizontal integration adds time and cost to the overall production of the product. This cost amplifies in case the organisation needs to handle hazardous material, like slug, etc. that are generated during product manufacturing. The overall cycle of conceptualization, design, prototype, and production via subtraction strategy is costly and time-consuming. This strategy also limits the evaluation of parallel concepts to solve a problem. The cost of evaluating multiple prototypes with this approach is a huge hindrance. Future of work invention must turn things upside down from a strategy perspective.

To:

Addition. Imagine a "boat" being printed as soon as the "print" command is fired from the computer. Yes, a real boat. You are correct, 3D printing is the technology that does this magic. The most exclusive part of this technology is the additive strategy instead of subtractive. In the context of Michelangelo's example, with this approach, when the design is done on digital medium, the conversion to physical or real medium occurs layer over layer to obtain the actual product. Because the approach is additive in nature, at each layer of product printing, the wastage is bare minimum. And yes, the material chosen for printing is reusable, say plastic or an eco-friendly artificial compound. Future of work sees time as money. With this approach, as the time to realization of a product is reduced, the overall profit cycle is accelerated. This also gives the organisation short windows to evaluate multiple design options to choose the best prototype for solving the problem. You will be surprised to know that the term *stereo lithography* was coined in 1984 by Chuck Hull. It is one of the types of technology that are employed to create models and parts using photochemical processes. You must be thinking that if the technology was is available since 30 years, why is it not widely adopted. And here comes the distinction between invention and innovation. The invention and adoption of rapid printing technique requires process, policy, and mindset change. Future of work strategy across industries will see accelerated adoption of rapid printing technology. The designer of the future of work product will sit in, say, Europe and design on their computer. They will press the print button to realise the product. And the product will immediately be printed somewhere in Asia or America continent. Once this printed prototype is validated for scale, the print command can be given for thousands of units together instead of one. So, what is stopping your organisation to turn the "print purpose" upside down, if not done so already for future of work?

Words of wisdom:

Tangible "Future of work" product generation strategies will be built on "additive" principle.

Future of work organisations MUST be quick to prototype the ideas for trial. This will reduce the time to market, make the organisation green, and reduce the overhead cost to handle the waste produced in the production line. The cost, time, and quality delay of raw material shipment will also be reduced as the product can be manufactured at scale near the source of production of raw material.

37

DISTINCT DAWN

From:

Retire. The lifecycle of work in the last century was very well-defined -get certified by an institution with a degree, get into an organisation, stick to a career ladder, work for 40 years, and then, retire at the age of 65. After retirement, an individual lived for a few decades before retiring from life. The "Pension", and in most cases, the government "health care plan" could take care of the financial and health needs of a retiree. The age of 65 was a lighthouse, right from day 0 of work. The end of age of 65 was like a curtain being pulled on the work life of a stage show. Not sure if this justifies the very well-known saying, *"All the world's a stage"*.And one works on stage till the age of 65. This lifecycle model has been followed by millions of people on this earth. The capitalisation, industrialisation, and trade centres have created enough, and in certain cases, more than wealth for many individuals during this time. This rise in wealth has increased the life expectancy of humans from 48 years in 1950 to 72.2 years in 2017. With increase in human population and life expectancy, the pension and health care system came under severe burden to support the number of people who retire. So, in the past decade or half, if one retired at the age of 60 or 65, the question that they had to answer was are they sufficiently funded to live the rest of their retirement life? Do you know the ratio of yes to no for this question?

To:

Retry. With "no pension" becoming the norm, and increasein longevity, the employees of the future of work are evolving to a new workstyle. The increasing inflation, cost of living, cost of healthcare, and commodities have put a huge pressure on the current saving basket of employees. And necessity is the mother of invention. The gig economy started seeing opportunities to give people multiple retirements, instead of one. No more is it one "sunset" of the work life of an individual. Instead, there could be three or four seasons of work life. No longer can one drive after paying for a car, in the gig economy, anyone can get paid for driving a car at their own wish. No longer can one pay for food and then eat the food, in the gig economy, anyone can deliver the food to earn their own bread. The future of work is giving the opportunity to "retry" instead of "retiring". No more do the individuals have to spend a long time to earn a certificate to start earning, they can earn their bread by learning quickly, often online. Also, instead of having their liquidity put into assets, the future of work employees are creating multiple income streams. For example, the employees of future of work are not putting money in buying houses using mortgage. The future of work employees are instead investing in stocks or start-ups to increase their liquidity.

Words of wisdom:

"Future of work" will make "Pension" a thing of past.

Future of work employees will seize the opportunity as they evolve. The skilling, un-skilling, and re-skilling will be a continuous nature of employees of future of work. This will ensure that one employee will be adept at more than one skill over the period of tenure of work.

APPENDIX

- **Five pillars of Future of Work Growth Principles**
  To create your future of work. The below framework is the guiding principal to start on your and your organisation's journey today. Connect, protect and add the dots in your continuous evolving journey of Future of Work. This MUST be done on a periodic basis that is comfortable for you.

Why work? (Challenges)	Experience of work? (Feelings)	How do we work? (Structure)	Tools for Work? (Tools)	Purpose of work? (What gets you/your people out of bed every day?)
Digital Real estate	Space	Organized	Integral Intangible	Exquisite
estate	Sensitive	Organisation	Data-Driven	Experience
Ideal Identity	Location	Tactical Tasks	Distributed	Jobs to
Intermittent	Limit	9 to 5	Systems	Careers
Internet	Creativity	Real to virtual	Cumbersome Code	Inclusive
Privacy	Craft	(PA to RPA)	Assertive Ambient	Intent
Problems	Dress	Hold to Hire	Modern Machines	Global
Super	Dilemma		Consistent Cloud	Gesture
Humans	Original		Emotion	Green Goal
	Outcome		Environment	Monday
			Server to	Motivation
			Server-less	Purpose
			Security Scenario	Print
			Growing G (3-4-5)	Distinct
			Quantum Quest	Dawn
			Simple Software	(retire)
			Prototype	
			Production	

Future of Work evolution Template – Four Stage evolution

- Task 1 – Old way of doing things
- Task 2 – New way of doing things

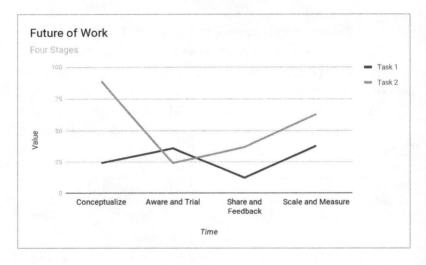

REFERENCES

- Events that changed the world - Rodney Castleden

- https://www.statista.com/statistics/617136/digital-population-worldwide/

- https://www.scientificamerican.com/article/the-quantum-internet-is-emerging-one-experiment-at-a-time/ (quantum networks)

- Moon vs. Ghetto, Richard R. Nelson: https://www.youtube.com/watch?v=KfL27L29l20

- https://en.wikipedia.org/wiki/Timeline_of_computing_1980%E2%80%931989#1980

- https://www.weforum.org/agenda/2020/06/renewable-energy-cheaper-coal/

- https://en.wikipedia.org/wiki/Stereolithography

ABOUT THE AUTHOR

Prashant Pandey, known as Aki-san in Japan, is an inventor, technologist and mentor. Learn, share and care are his values. His mission is to apply emerging technology to solve business problems and improve lives. He has lived, worked and earned in USA, Canada, Israel, India and Singapore.

Professionally, he helps clients to build the future of work to transform their security, productivity and employee experience. He is a passionate emerging technology leader and evangelist with proven records in embedded systems development, enterprise and technology architecture design.

Academically, IIM Calcutta, India taught him executive sales and marketing management. NIT Patna, India made him Electronics and Communications Engineer. Science College, Patna strengthened his science and mathematics fundamentals. Manoj Vasudevan, world champion of public speaking & Toast Masters International Club, Singapore taught him Public Speaking.

He shares his innovation and technology expertise with emerging founders at startup-o.com, Asia's leading startup nurturing platform. He already has contributed to the cause of education and wants to touch 1000 lives by supporting their education and mentoring.

For fun, he reads, rides bike and travels. He is married to an engineer and entrepreneur wife, Supriya. Supriya and he have a son, "Sparsh" and they live in Singapore.

****

Social Links:

Startup-o: https://www.startup-o.com/portfolio-item/prashant/

Twitter: pandey_prash

Website: www.prashantpandeyofficial.com

Linkedin: https://www.linkedin.com/in/prashant-pandey-aka-aki-san-aab2742/